Putting Together Professional Portfolios

Putting Together
Professional Portfolios

Christine Forde, Margery McMahon
and Jenny Reeves

Los Angeles • London • New Delhi • Singapore • Washington DC

© Christine Forde, Margery McMahon and Jenny Reeves 2009
First published 2009

Apart from any fair dealing for the purposes of
research or private study, or criticism or review, as
permitted under the Copyright, Designs and Patents Act,
1988, this publication may be reproduced, stored or
transmitted in any form, or by any means, only with
the prior permission in writing of the publishers,
or in the case of reprographic reproduction, in accordance
with the terms of licences issued by the Copyright Licensing
Agency. Enquiries concerning reproduction outside those
terms should be sent to the publishers.

SAGE Publications Ltd
1 Oliver's Yard
55 City Road
London EC1Y 1SP

SAGE Publications Inc.
2455 Teller Road
Thousand Oaks, California 91320

SAGE Publications India Pvt Ltd
B 1/I 1 Mohan Cooperative Industrial Area
Mathura Road
New Delhi 110 044

SAGE Publications Asia-Pacific Pte Ltd
33 Pekin Street #02-01
Far East Square
Singapore 048763

Library of Congress Control Number: 2008927609

British Library Cataloguing in Publication data

A catalogue record for this book is available from the British Library

ISBN 978-1-4129-4669-8
ISBN 978-1-4129-4670-4 (pbk)

Typeset by C&M Digitals (P) Ltd., Chennai, India
Printed in Great Britain by CPI Antony Rowe, Chippenham, Wiltshire
Printed on paper from sustainable resources

Contents

About the Authors

Christine Forde is a Professor of Leadership and Professional Learning in the Faculty of Education at Glasgow University. During her career, she has worked as a primary teacher and a tutor in Initial Teacher Education, but most recently has been involved in working with serving teachers on a variety of professional development programmes including the Scottish Qualification for Headship (SQH). She works mainly in the areas of leadership and management in schools and in teacher professional development and learning and has published a number of books and articles on teacher professional development with her two co-authors, most recently *Professional Development, Reflection and Enquiry* (Paul Chapman, 2006) with Margery McMahon and other colleagues. She is involved with colleagues in research projects looking at preparation programmes for headship and the recruitment and retention of head teachers. In addition, she has published books in the area of gender and education and feminist perspectives on education: *Feminist Utopianism and Education* (Sense Publishers, 2007).

Margery McMahon is Programme Director of the MEd in Professional Development, Reflection and Enquiry (Chartered Teacher Programme) at the University of Glasgow. With a background in History and Politics, she has worked as a Lecturer in Politics, as a teacher of History and Politics and as Head of a History Department. In her main role in the Faculty of Education she oversees the Chartered Teacher programme and teaches on a number of its courses. She has published several articles on professional development and professional learning and was co-author with Christine Forde and other colleagues of *Professional Development, Reflection and Enquiry* (Paul Chapman, 2006). She has been involved in research projects relating to Teachers' Working Time and the Impact of Chartered Teacher and is currently involved in a research project on Programmes for Headship and a project on Intercultural Professional Development. Her roots in History and Politics are sustained by contributing to courses on Educational Policy and Globalization and researching and writing about Northern Ireland. Her latest book is *Government and Politics of Northern Ireland* (Colourpoint Publishers, 2008).

Jenny Reeves is Director of Continuing Professional Development at the Institute of Education at the University of Stirling. Her particular research interests lie in the dynamics and impact of practice-focused learning and sense-making processes in, and across, organisational boundaries and she has published a number of articles relating to these topics. She has published two books in 2008: *Practice-Based Learning: Developing Excellence in Teaching* (Dunedin Press), co-edited with Alison Fox, and *Educating Experienced Teachers: Exploring the Social Dynamics of Professional Knowledge Transfer and Creation* (Springer). She also has a chapter in *Changing Teacher Professionalism*, edited by Sharon Gewirtz and Pat Mahony (Routledge, 2008). Recent research projects include looking at the outcomes of practice-based approaches to leadership development in South Africa and Scotland, working in partnership with a local authority using organisational learning as a strategy for school improvement and continuing exploration of issues of practice and knowledge transfer and creation in relation to Chartered Teachers, including working with Margery McMahon on the Impact of Chartered Teacher project.

Preface

This book has its origins in our work with educational practitioners on programmes for continuing professional development. Each of us is involved in a number of professional development courses for teachers and school leaders who are working towards professional qualifications and academic awards. In these programmes, portfolios are used as a tool to chart the development of the professional practice of the practitioner and to aid critical reflection. This work raised for us a number of significant questions, particularly about the relationship between development and professional practice, which we have gone on to investigate through different research projects. In this book we draw widely from both our teaching and research to explore the purposes and principles underpinning the development of professional portfolios and to provide practical advice about how to design and build a portfolio.

We would like to thank our colleagues at the University of Glasgow, the University of Stirling and the Western SQH Consortium, who have very much been part of the development of the approaches discussed in this book. Particular thanks goes to Dr Brian Canavan, University of Glasgow, for his input in relation to electronic portfolios and for agreeing to the inclusion of his professional portfolio as an exemplar. Finally, we would also like to thank the many participants on the various professional development programmes whose questions and suggestions have helped us refine our ideas.

Christine Forde
Margery McMahon
Jenny Reeves

How to Use This Book

There are many reasons why you as an educational practitioner are considering embarking on the task of developing a portfolio but at the heart of all of these reasons lies our understanding of what it means to be a professional, that is, to be a practitioner who seeks to develop and extend their practice for the benefit of learners. Improving and reviewing the professional performance of teachers and other educational practitioners is a major issue across all education sectors and so emphasis is placed on continuing professional development and accreditation. However, it is important that educational practitioners develop their skill and sense of agency in looking closely and finding ways of improving their practice and a portfolio provides a framework for this. Portfolios are created by teachers and other educational practitioners either as part of a programme of study or as an ongoing record of their opportunities for professional development. These examples of portfolios can be described as 'professional portfolios' where the distinctive feature is the relationship between the learning and practice of the educational professional.

You may be working in an early years establishment, a primary or secondary school or within tertiary education. In each of these sectors, there are numerous examples of portfolios being used as part of professional development. Portfolios are a common feature in the range of professional programmes such as Chartered Teacher in Scotland, as well as professional qualifications in preparation for headship. Portfolios are also used as part of becoming an accredited teacher in higher education. You may be involved in one of these or a similar programme that leads to an academic or professional qualification, or you may be keeping a portfolio as a professional review and appraisal tool, or you might be maintaining a portfolio as a career development activity. Whatever your starting point and professional context, in this book you will find material that will provide guidance as you go about the task of planning and building your professional portfolio. This book will enable you to:

- design and plan a portfolio

- chart and analyse relevant professional experiences

- identify your professional development needs

- plan your learning to develop your practice

- assess your performance against standards and competences frameworks

- reflect critically on your practice

- present evidence of your practice and achievements

- plan your future development.

Outline of chapters

Chapter 1: What Is a Portfolio?

We explore the idea of a 'professional portfolio' and examine several different examples of professional portfolios developed by educational practitioners.

Chapter 2: Professional Learning

We consider different ways of exploring the professional learning of educational practitioners. We look at the use of standards, competences frameworks and benchmarks to plan and then reflect on professional learning which can be used to shape a professional portfolio.

Chapter 3: Writing a Professional Autobiography

We look at the development of a professional autobiography as a way of beginning the process of self-evaluation which is a key element of a professional portfolio. We examine ways of using a professional autobiography to chart your development over your career as an educator.

Chapter 4: Action Learning

We explore the concept of 'action learning' and how it can be used in the continuing professional development of educational practitioners. We look at different spheres for learning such as self, organisation and the wider educational environment and ways of planning learning.

Chapter 5: Reflection as Learning

We consider the place of reflection in the continuing professional development of educational practitioners and explore ways of using reflection to review and enhance practice.

Chapter 6: Recording Learning and Practice

We focus on the question of providing evidence of professional development and learning. Here we examine two critical issues: what is 'evidence of learning' and what makes 'good' evidence.

Chapter 7: Describing and Reflecting on Practice

We look at what we mean by 'critically reflective writing'. We explore a framework for different levels of reflective writing and different strategies to generate ideas.

Chapter 8: Designing an Electronic Portfolio

We examine the use of e-portfolios: some of the advantages and possibilities in using an e-format and ways of avoiding some of the pitfalls. Examples of the design of e-portfolios are included to enable you to plan and construct e-portfolios.

Chapter 9: Designing and Constructing Your Portfolio

In this final chapter we draw together a number of the key ideas explored in the previous chapters and consider ways of designing and constructing your professional portfolio through which you can plan and demonstrate your professional development as an educational practitioner.

A learning cycle

The chapters in this book are sequenced to follow the process of learning underpinning the design and construction of a portfolio. We move from the process of self-evaluation and the identification of needs to planning learning experiences and then on to charting and reflecting on practice and development.

Each of the chapters in this book has a number of key questions and practical tasks to enable you to apply the principles to your own professional portfolio whatever format you wish or need to adopt. You will find here:

- examples of work

- practical activities for individuals and groups

- summaries and checklists

A note about terminology

In this book we are examining the process by which practitioners can design and construct a 'professional portfolio' to chart their development as a professional. As portfolios are used by practitioners across all sectors of education, we have used the term 'educational practitioner' or 'practitioner' rather than the more specific term 'teacher' unless we are discussing a particular example from a school context.

1

What Is a Portfolio?

In this introductory chapter we discuss what we mean by 'a professional portfolio'. We explore different models of portfolios and consider ways these might be used to support professional development.

Key ideas

- **Why develop a portfolio?**
- **What is a professional portfolio?**
- **Different models of a professional portfolio**
- **Looking at the contents of a portfolio**
- **Portfolio-based learning**
- **Key questions to plan your portfolio**

Why develop a professional portfolio?

Central to the process of developing a portfolio is our understanding of what it means to be a learning professional, that is, someone who continues to develop and enhance their skills and understanding for the benefit of the learners they work with. A professional portfolio provides a space in which you can plan and reflect in depth on your practice, helping you identify your strengths and find ways of building on these.

What is a professional portfolio?

There are many different ways in which a portfolio can be developed and we explore different constructions of portfolios, ranging from prescriptive formats to open-ended frameworks. Underpinning the use of portfolios in professional development are some common principles related to how practitioners learn and develop their professional practice throughout their careers. We contextualise these principles by drawing directly from the experience of teachers, school leaders and lecturers in tertiary education who have developed professional portfolios across a range of professional development programmes, and from current research on portfolio-based learning and assessment. We also look at the design and construction of e-portfolios as the use of these is becoming more common in professional development programmes.

In broad terms, a professional portfolio could be described as a collection of material put together in a meaningful way to demonstrate the practice and learning of an educational practitioner. Portfolios are used for different purposes and vary in the way they are designed and constructed. Most portfolios are built up over a period of time, though even this may vary in length, with some portfolios created in a concentrated way over a short period of time, often as part of a programme of study. Other portfolios are maintained and regularly updated as the practitioner moves through his/her career. However, a professional portfolio is not a random collection of material and artefacts. The items relate to what the practitioner sees as important in the development of his/her practice, whether this is in a classroom, seminar room, school or wider educational setting. The format of portfolios also varies in the way items are gathered and then presented. The key issue here is that the design and presentation of the portfolio makes sense to the practitioner and anyone else who might read this, such as a critical friend, tutor or line manager.

What are the benefits and challenges of developing a professional portfolio?

Designing and building a professional portfolio is a powerful means of planning, enhancing and reviewing practice. Here are some of the benefits of producing a professional portfolio identified by participants on different professional development programmes. Developing the portfolio:

- created a sense of achievement

- built my self-confidence

- was an opportunity to conduct an in-depth self-evaluation

- developed my skills of reflection

- developed greater awareness of the context I work in

- made me think about where I want to go and what I need to develop

- strengthened my understanding of my development as a practitioner

- gave more rigour in analysing my practice

- created a sense of my own journey as a professional

- allowed me to become more critical

- let me appreciate some of my successes more

- helped me know and be confident about my strengths

- enabled me to think about my practice and ways I can develop this.

Clearly, producing a professional portfolio has benefits personally for an educational practitioner by building confidence and greater understanding as well as other benefits, with the educational practitioner looking in depth at his/her practice and then finding ways to improve this. However, there are some challenges. Among the issues identified by course participants are:

- the portfolio could become simply a paper trail

- constructing and assembling the portfolio is time-consuming

- very 'messy' at the start when trying to find a format

- the portfolio can create an atomistic approach – looking at different tasks without making connections

- the portfolio can focus on the functional aspects of practice without looking at the 'big picture'.

In this book we seek to enable you to derive benefit from the process of designing and constructing your portfolio by providing a range of techniques and examples that will also help you avoid some of these pitfalls.

Why do you want to develop a portfolio?

The first issue to consider is the purpose of your portfolio, so we will begin by exploring some of the different purposes and then relate these to the design principles and formats of different types of portfolios commonly used in education.

 **Key Question**

Why do you want to develop a portfolio?

There are many reasons why you might be developing a portfolio. Is it:

- a contractual obligation: perhaps as part of a professional review and appraisal process

- for an academic or professional award where developing a portfolio is part of the learning and assessment process

- part of a professional development programme where a portfolio is the means to review practice and plan further professional development?

Is the purpose of your portfolio:

- to illustrate achievements

- to demonstrate ongoing development of thinking and practice

- to collect evidence

- to provide a vehicle for reflection?

Your reasons for developing a portfolio will provide some broad parameters for you to begin the process of designing the format and deciding on the contents.

 Task: Thinking about why you want to develop a portfolio
Jot down some reasons and think about how these might shape your portfolio.

Different models of a professional portfolio

There are many different types of professional portfolios used in continuing development of educational practitioners. Some portfolios are very structured while others are far looser in their design and contents. In some programmes there are clear guidelines to which the practitioner must adhere; in others, practitioners can determine the size, scope, format and contents of the portfolio. There are advantages and disadvantages to both structured portfolios and to more open-ended portfolios.

Portfolios with prescribed structures are evident in programmes leading to a professional qualification or an academic award where the portfolio forms part of the assessment of these programmes. Increasingly these programmes use a competence framework or standard and the portfolio is the means to demonstrate the achievement of the areas of practice specified in a particular framework. The guidelines are useful in helping you design the shape and scope of your portfolio and helping you to plan the activities you must undertake and decide how to gather the relevant evidence. However, such tight guidelines can also be limiting as there is little scope for you to examine areas of practice and to add materials that have a special significance for your development within your professional context.

At the other end of the continuum, with open-ended portfolios the choice is very much shaped by what the practitioner sees as meaningful and important. This is a considerable strength of this type of portfolio because it allows you scope in exploring and presenting what you see as meaningful and what you regard as your strengths and successes. However, this greater flexibility makes the task of designing and building a portfolio more complex. These types of portfolios are more challenging because you are being asked to make decisions about what you see as relevant and important to your development. Some practitioners might see this as daunting while others will relish the challenge.

Is your portfolio open-ended, in which you have scope:

- to choose the documents and artefacts

- to decide on the design and presentation of the portfolio?

Is your portfolio clearly structured, in which you have to include:

- specific items of evidence to illustrate aspects of professional practice

- specific formats for the presentation of the portfolio?

 Task: Let's consider your portfolio
Use the questions above to map out the broad parameters of your portfolio.

In practice, probably most portfolios used by educational practitioners are a mixture: there are guidelines for the broad format and contents but there is some scope to allow practitioners to shape either the format or the contents of a portfolio to reflect better their own circumstances and practice. We can see this in the different portfolios we look at now.

Looking at different portfolios

We will illustrate the differences in the purposes and design of portfolios by drawing from our work on a number of development programmes. Here we look at different formats of several portfolios. We will look in more detail at specific elements of a portfolio in later chapters.

Portfolio A is taken from a masters programme taught by one of the authors in the USA. Here participants were undertaking a course on a cross-curricular approach to the development of expressive arts. The participants were from all sectors of education and included a number of special needs support assistants. As part of the assessment each participant was asked to compile a portfolio recording and reflecting on their own development in expressive arts throughout the programme. This is an example of a portfolio that uses course work built up during the programme.

Portfolio B represents the current practice in many schools in the UK where staff maintain a record of the professional development opportunities they have been involved in over the course of a school year.

Portfolio C is from a professional qualification for aspiring headteachers where participants lead a major school development project. As part of the assessment of the programme participants develop a portfolio of evidence charting the process and outcomes of the project and reflect critically on their own learning.

Portfolio D is from a programme in which teachers can seek accreditation as an accomplished teacher. Teachers must present a portfolio to demonstrate their practice in specific aspects of teaching and learning. The teachers can opt to present their work as an e-portfolio.

Portfolio E is from an action research programme set up by a local authority in which staff complete a portfolio to record the process and outcomes of the project and subsequently the portfolio is available for other staff members to use.

We will now look at the contents of each of these portfolios. Although each portfolio is linked to the professional development of the educational practitioner, there are some significant differences and we will look at how these determine the design and contents of the portfolios.

What is in a professional portfolio?

There is considerable variation in how the portfolios are presented and types of materials included in these different portfolios.

Portfolio A: Course portfolio

A key outcome of the first part of the course was the development of the participants' confidence, enthusiasm and skill in expressive arts. The design of this portfolio is very like the portfolios used by artists and architects to present their work. Participants were asked to collect any items that had been significant in their development in expressive arts during the programme, including artefacts and materials they had created themselves. These were then presented in a portfolio with a short commentary in their learning log explaining the significance of each item.

Course portfolio

- course outline and learning plan
- a learning log maintained during the programme
- a tape of music composed by the participant
- a montage the participant produced
- a short digital film of the process of making the montage
- photographs of her own art work
- a poem used as a starting point for two short prose texts written by the participant
- two examples of her own artwork – a pencil drawing and a cloth hanging
- a small sketchbook
- a reflection on the programme

Portfolio B: CPD portfolio

As part of the school's policy, all staff maintain a record of their continuing professional development (CPD). In the guidelines all teachers are asked to (1) keep a record for the professional development activities they have engaged in over the year, (2) reflect on their development as preparation for their annual review and (3) complete a written evaluation for any professional development course they attend in or out of school. The evaluation form asks staff also to identify what actions they have taken as a result of this professional development.

CPD Portfolio

- a self-evaluation form for the professional review interview
- agreed plan of action for the coming year
- a list of professional development activities and dates
- three evaluation reports on courses attended
- attendance certificates and notes from courses
- the agreed reports of previous professional reviews

Portfolio C: Competence-based portfolio

An important aspect of the professional qualification for aspiring headteachers is the school-based project in which the participants take forward a whole school development project. The portfolio is the final assessment task. The structure of the portfolio is based on the competence framework and the contents are specified: the aspiring headteachers present a portfolio of evidence and a critical commentary illustrating their achievement of the different elements of a competence framework through their work in leading the school-based project. The framework maps out the core management tasks and personal qualities of a headteacher.

Competence-based portfolio

- introduction and outline of the school context
- outline of the structure of the portfolio
- project plan
- claims for competence matched against the core functions of leadership
- an index of the evidence
- items of evidence linked to the competence framework
- critical reflective commentary

Portfolio D: Portfolio for the accreditation of prior learning

This portfolio is from a postgraduate programme also based on a standard. The standard here maps out the different aspects of 'accomplished teaching' and specifies a number of professional actions the teacher must demonstrate. As part of the assessment process the teacher must build a portfolio of evidence illustrating the activities undertaken and the impact of these on the learning and achievement of pupils in the class. This enables the teacher to demonstrate how they have met the various elements of the competence framework through a series of case studies. There is a clear specification for the portfolio and a set of assessment criteria but participants can opt to present their work in an e-portfolio.

Accreditation e-portfolio

- plan for developing a claim
- short digital video illustrating the context of the classroom
- PowerPoint illustrating in graph form baseline assessment data
- examples of e-learning materials
- examples of pupil work and achievement
- e-journal on project
- PowerPoint presentation with photographs and audio commentary on the accomplishment of each professional action specified in the competence framework
- critical reflection on the process of professional learning

---

Portfolio E: Project portfolio

A group of teachers from a local school cluster have been working together with a university tutor on an action research project to improve attainment in mathematics. The teachers have been sponsored by their local authority and given time for the work to be conducted and for the group to meet together as well as a small budget to buy resources and materials. Teachers are expected to maintain a portfolio throughout the project which is discussed regularly with the project leader and their school co-ordinator. At the end of the project the portfolio is finalised and a copy submitted to provide materials and guidance on the mathematics project and on action research for other teachers in the associated schools.

Project portfolio

- project plan
- baseline data
- research report
- resource materials
- guidelines on research methodologies
- reflections on the process of the action research project
- materials used in the project
- PowerPoint presentation to teachers

There are some common features shared by these portfolios, but there are also some significant differences.

 Task: What similarities and differences do you see between these sample portfolios?

Make a note of some of the similarities and differences between these five sample portfolios.

First steps in planning

These portfolios have been chosen because they help illustrate the range of portfolios used by educational practitioners. The next step is for you to consider how one or more of these examples relate to your portfolio.

 Key Question

How do some of these portfolios match what is required in your portfolio?

There is a variety of reasons why an educational practitioner might want to develop a portfolio but underpinning all of these are some common principles. Although in each example the portfolio has been developed for a different purpose, there are some common features. Portfolio components typically include four broad types of materials:

- *Planning:* planning is an important element in all portfolios, whether this is the planning of project work or professional development activities. Plans are also included in portfolios for the accreditation of prior learning where the practitioner will draw up a plan to construct his/her portfolio based on personal experiences and accomplishments and possibly address any additional areas needed to meet all the requirements of a particular programme.

- *Description:* the outline and description of the area or areas of practice is important so there is a clear and accurate account of the activities the practitioner has undertaken.

- *Evidence:* documentary evidence, testimonies and artefacts that illustrate what the professional practitioner did and achieved. This can include such items as curricular materials, pupils' work, artefacts produced, professional development materials, documents from a school project, learning resources and, increasingly, digital resources.

- *Reflection:* reflection is a vital part of the portfolio, in which the professional practitioner reviews and critically appraises his/her practice and experiences. The length of these reflections will vary, but this is an important element in portfolio-based learning.

 Task: Planning the timescale for the development of your portfolio

Create an initial time plan for the development of your portfolio, building in time for self-evaluation and undertaking any activities, creating a structure for the portfolio, gathering evidence and reflecting on your development as an educational practitioner.

Thinking about these questions will help you to move from the task of producing a portfolio to considering a wider set of activities associated with portfolio-based learning.

Portfolio-based learning

Designing a portfolio is a demanding task and we have to be concerned that this does not become simply an administrative task of gathering different pieces of paper. Instead, the process of designing and constructing a portfolio itself should be a valuable learning experience. It becomes a tool to promote reflection and deeper learning. In portfolio-based learning the educator plans, collects and reflects on the process of their own development as a professional practitioner. The portfolio is constructed in a dynamic way, with items being collected, reviewed and refined over a period of time. Some portfolios may continue to the completion of a particular programme while others may be maintained across the span of a practitioner's career.

Designing a professional portfolio

Portfolios are increasingly being used in professional and academic qualifications in which portfolios are used as part of the assessment process to provide 'evidence' of the achievements and learning of the educator. Frequently the portfolio, or at least some of the elements of the portfolio, become the topic of discussion and reflection with a critical friend or colleague. Working with a critical friend, mentor or tutor can provide feedback useful for the development of the portfolio and which will also serve to deepen your understanding of the principles underpinning your practice.

How you go about the task of designing and building your portfolio is important:

- Will this be a portfolio that you develop and complete at the end of a programme or is it something that is maintained and reviewed throughout the programme?

- Is the design and construction of the portfolio something you will be doing by yourself or are there opportunities to reflect on the process and contents with other practitioners or with a tutor?

 Task: Working with others

Jot down some of the people with whom you might discuss the development of your portfolio.

Stages in the development of your portfolio

In designing and building a portfolio, a practitioner has to decide what has been important in his/her practice, what the successes have been, what areas might be enhanced or improved. This process of reflection is central to both structured portfolios based on a competence framework and to more open-ended portfolios. If you are using a competence framework you have to consider how you achieved these broad areas in the specific context of your own establishment: what does it mean, for example, to lead learning in your school or department? If it is a more open-ended portfolio you have to determine what has been important and how you might demonstrate what you have achieved. For both types of portfolios you are reviewing, evaluating and, most importantly, making sense of your own experiences and professional practice.

There are then a number of key questions you have to consider as you begin the process of developing a portfolio, which we will consider in greater depth in later chapters in this book.

- *Planning*: how you can plan your learning to take account of the important dimensions of your professional learning in your work context.

- *Practice*: the frameworks you can use to chart your own practice and development.

- *Gathering and selecting evidence*: selection of relevant and appropriate evidence.

- *Reflecting:* ways you can reflect critically on your practice and development.

Summary: Setting out the parameters of your portfolio

In this chapter we have looked at some of the issues you have to consider as you begin the process of developing a portfolio. Here are a number of questions designed to help you set out some broad parameters for the project.

Purpose and audience

- Why are you developing a portfolio?
- Who is the audience: is there more than one; do they have different requirements?

Design of the portfolio

- Is the portfolio paper-based or electronic?
- Are there any restrictions in terms of length?
- Is there a competence framework or a set of criteria that must be used?

Contents of the portfolio

What kind of material can be included:

- text
- visual material
- digital material
- artefacts?

Recording and reflecting on learning

Does the portfolio include:

- a description of event and/achievements
- evidence of performance
- reflection?

2

Professional Learning

A portfolio is a means of structuring, demonstrating and reflecting on your development as a professional. At the heart of portfolio development is your learning. As a starting point in this chapter we consider the idea of 'professional learning. We will explore the question of what professional learning looks like and how you can begin to think about making claims about your development which can then be shaped for your professional portfolio.

Key ideas

- What it means to be a professional
- Defining professional learning
- Definitions of professional learning in policy
- Models of professional learning and development
- Using models to evaluate and plan learning

Being a professional

In this chapter we consider what is meant by 'professional learning' and look at a range of strategies you might adopt. We begin by considering the term 'professional'. Then we consider the contribution of portfolio-based learning to your development as a professional. A portfolio is a demonstration of the process and outcomes of your development as an educational practitioner. Therefore a key issue is the process of your learning.

A profession is often defined as an occupation requiring special training and, as a consequence, we tend to think of professionals as people who are particularly competent at what they do. They provide us with services on the basis of having specialist knowledge about their area of practice and their capacity to use this specialist knowledge to our benefit. On these grounds we assign them the power to make decisions about us and recommend courses of action for us to follow. Thus we expect those with a claim to professionalism to be trustworthy. Professionals have a responsibility to promote the wellbeing of those they work with. This is particularly obvious in the case of the medical profession, where doctors are required to undertake an oath to do no harm to their patients. Equally, lawyers and teachers are expected to take moral responsibility for their interactions with clients and students and to work in the latter's best interests.

Task: Thinking about professionalism

Look at this extract taken from an interview with someone about their best teacher. In what ways does it exemplify the kind of professionalism we have outlined?

'I had the English teacher I really needed. She would sit me down with an essay that I'd thought was rather good and show me the sort of essay I should be writing, and what I should be reading, the difference between literary criticism and studying someone's work for your own advancement. I learned how to look at literature in such a way that I could enter it, pick out the techniques in works I admired and see why they worked.'

Extracts taken from 'My Best Teacher', *The Times Educational Supplement,* 9 August 2002. Daniel Handley was talking to Geraldine Brennan

The interview extract sums up the core of what it means to be an educational professional. We can see how the teacher developed a positive relationship, held high expectations to foster the skills, understanding and confidence of their pupil to enable them to achieve in their learning and be successful. As we expect that professionals will act in the best interests of their clients, we also expect them to be committed to continually improving the service they provide and to ensuring they make use of best practice in their interactions with us and on our behalf. In order to achieve this they should be drawing upon both their own experience and the accumulated knowledge of their profession as a collective. In turn, they should be contributing to the further development of their profession by engaging in dialogue about matters of professional practice with their colleagues.

Underlying these expectations is a notion of accountability which professionals have:

- to the people they work with – patients, clients and students – which entails a duty of care

- to their professional colleagues as a collective

- to the organisation in which they are employed.

Professionals work under circumstances where they are assisting a range of people in a variety of different contexts. Therefore, in order to achieve certain goals they need to be able to continually adjust what they do. Professionals work on the basis of being responsive to particular cases rather than routinely working under a set of stable circumstances. Professionals are expected to exercise sound judgement in complex situations. For instance, when my child goes to school her teacher may be working with a class of 20 to 30 children but I still expect that teacher to get to know my child and respond to her particular learning needs.

To summarise, we expect professionals to:

- have a sound knowledge of their field of practice

- base their practice on ethical principles

- understand people and respond to their needs.

Professional action, knowledge and professional identity

We have placed expertise at the heart of our definition of what it is to be a professional, so in this sense we are privileging knowledge as a defining characteristic of professionalism. However, we have also indicated that we are not referring here to a simple framework of understanding because we are defining practitioner knowledge as an intimate mixture of three different elements:

- *Know why: t*he capacity to act in accordance with recognised ethical values such as social justice and agreed principles of practice for the profession.

- *Know what:* A knowledge of the techniques, tools and processes that can be used to address the needs of the client.

- *Know how:* The skills to be able to use the techniques, tools and processes (including an understanding of self), and the capacity to understand contexts and conditions in order to select the best approach in relation to each specific case.

On this basis, your judgement of what to do in a particular case is based upon *why* you should take a particular course of action, *what* the course of action should consist of and *how* you are going to carry it out. This mixture is not something that can be written down, as developers of expert systems have found to their cost, but something embodied in practitioners who must respond appropriately and effectively to the case before them.

These three elements can be used as a basis for self-evaluation and reflecting on what you have learned and what aspects of your practice you still require to develop. For instance, you can use the model to investigate your beliefs and assumptions and then look at what you do to see how far it mirrors your principles (see the task overleaf). In this way the three elements of professional action can be used as lenses to examine your professional actions and experience as shown in Figure 2.1.

By changing the questions you can use the same model to plan for developing your capacity for action:

- In what way should I act in this type of situation? (*Know why*)

- What approaches would be best? (*Know what*)

- Have I got the capability to carry them out? (*Know how*)

Professional identity

This definition of professional practice obviously raises the issue of professional identity. If your effectiveness is tied up in who you are and in your integrity then your personal qualities are a key element of your practice and your personal development is an important part of your learning. Professional judgement is a mixture of the practical and the ethical and is something that is developed as part of personal experience. It draws on knowledge developed from your personal experience of a variety of contexts and your knowledge of yourself. As professional practice is so dependent on your judgement, your personal professional

Figure 2.1   Three elements of practice

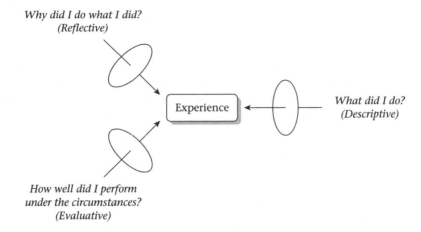

identity and the principles and values that underpin it are a critical element in terms of developing your practice.

 Task: Thinking about yourself as a professional

How would you describe yourself as a professional? What do you see as the most important aspects of your role as an educator? What values and beliefs shape your practice in these areas?

Lifelong learning and professional development

There has been an increasing emphasis on professional development recently in relation to policy in the public services. This is justified on the grounds that the changing circumstances brought about by globalisation and the growth in information technology require that we transform our approach to the delivery and nature of professional services. Rather than leaving professional learning to trial and error after a period of initial training, as often used to be the case, there is now an emphasis upon deliberately fostering continuing professional development throughout one's career. This is reflected in a focus on 'lifelong learning'. Professional development is usually described as falling into four broad categories:

- *Learning how to learn: reflective practice.* This represents a change in emphasis away from regarding professional learning as solely a matter of attending training to seeing it as an integral part of practice. On this basis you need to equip yourself to learn by developing the habit of reflecting on your practice and that of your organisation and seeking the means to improve it.

- *Improving your knowledge base: evidence-informed practice.* There is a demand for improvement in the knowledge base of professionals enshrined in the idea that practice should be 'evidence-informed' and 'research-led'. As a result professional development is equated with forms of professional enquiry and the active engagement of practitioners in researching their own practice whilst drawing on the research of others. Obviously this ties in with the previous point since your capacity to undertake professional enquiry can be seen as part of learning to learn.

- *Learning together: collegiality.* There is a marked change with regard to professional autonomy in many professions, with an increased emphasis on collegiality and peer-to-peer learning. This is seen as essential to creating more vibrant, evidence-informed professions with greater commitment to accountability and transparency. Modern professionals should, on this basis, see themselves as part of 'a community of practice' which promotes the professional growth of all its members through engaging in professional dialogue and the sharing of expertise.

- *Learning to work across boundaries: collaboration.* The need to work across professional boundaries is receiving greater attention, particularly where the complex needs and problems of certain groups in the community require a more holistic approach to their resolution. This places increased demands on the capacity of professionals to communicate effectively with each other and challenges traditional notions of specialism and autonomy.

Finally, there is an increased consensus that the goal of professional learning and development is not simply about knowing for knowing's sake – it is about the improvement of practice. This concern with making an impact on practice the test of professional development is where professional portfolios come into play. A professional portfolio is a tool for providing evidence that you have learned to change and develop your practice in the context of your day-to-day work.

Changing professional practice

Given the way in which we have typified professional work, one of the problems with professional development is that, where practice is so bound to context, it is difficult to come up with general routines and practices that are applicable in every case. To be an effective practitioner you have to go beyond a simple technical competence that might be learned by showing and telling you how to carry out your work. Thus simple models of knowledge transfer, such as the idea that you could attend a presentation by a colleague about her good practice and then simply go and apply it in your own context, bear little relation to the reality of change. Changing your professional behaviour is not simply a matter of changing your mind (although that is an important part of the process).

Because you are the instrument of any change in practice your professional development will necessarily involve you in the trial of new techniques and approaches and their on-going refinement. Until you can absorb them into your daily work your new learning is not part of your practice. During this time, trying out the new technique will be disruptive of your normal routines and therefore the change will be much easier to achieve with active support from, and dialogue with, others. You also need to allow yourself sufficient time to learn because changing routines involves not only learning new behaviours, it also requires unpicking some of your old ones.

Task: Changing practice

Consider the case study that follows and make a note of all the changes that will need to take place in order for Sally to alter her practice. Does this match with your experience of developing practice?

Case Study: Changing practice

Sally has been used to organising her class so that pupils work individually. She now wants to involve her pupils in assessing one another's work in order to improve the quality of their writing. She hopes that deciding and discussing what makes for good creative writing with each other will help pupils to plan and evaluate their own work more effectively.

Sally will have to learn how to manage the class in order to allow peer assessment to happen because the new practice requires a fundamental alteration in roles and relationships:

(a) having pupils working with pupils for the first time; and
(b) having pupils, rather than herself, assessing work.

To do so involves changing both her own and her pupils' attitudes about what constitutes legitimate classroom activity. As well as persuading her pupils and herself of the educational value of the new approach, Sally will also have to develop the capability of the pupils to work together. They will also need to learn how to make assessments and explain their decisions. Parents may well be concerned if the new practice is not explained to them since it may violate their expectations of teacher/pupil and pupil/pupil relationships. The teacher's colleagues may also be sceptical, and if they are not working in the same way, the teacher's capacity to justify her new practice to pupils and parents will be weakened.

This example illustrates that changing your practice, and sustaining the change, is not just a matter for you as an individual. It also involves all of those you interact with in your work.

In the next section we consider how, given the complexities of professional growth, you can use various models to help you to begin to identify and shape what you have learned and also what you should consider doing next in terms of your further development.

Frameworks for professional learning

In this section we are going to consider three types of framework that can be used to think about your overall development. These frameworks are:

- The three elements model of practice

- The novice to expert continuum model

- Professional standards

The three elements model of practice

We have already looked at, and used, the three elements model of practice (Figure 2.1). Another way of labelling the elements that has been used to structure some professional standards is:

- professional values and principles (*why*)

- professional knowledge and understanding (technical knowledge) (*what*)

- professional skills and attributes (*how*).

This model can be used as a basis for looking at your overall development, or specific stages in your professional career or particular events in your experience, as well as serving as a basis for planning for your development.

The novice to expert continuum model

The second framework is based on research into the performance and perceptions of practitioners by Dreyfus and Dreyfus published in 1986. It outlines a linear progression from an initial engagement with practice to the level of fluency and flexibility that characterises the performance of established, expert practitioners. Professional performance is categorised at five levels:

1 *Novices* stick rigidly to the rules and plans they have been taught. They have little understanding, or even perception of situational factors. Their judgements tend therefore to be simplistic.

2 *Advanced beginners* are able to recognise and act upon some characteristics of situations but tend to give equal weight to each of these separately and tend not to be able to consider them in relation to each other.

3 *Competent practitioners* can deal with the multiple facets of practice and are beginning to develop a strategic and more integrated approach. They tend to deal with a limited number of standardised, routine behaviour sequences related to various aspects of the situation. Their decision-making is deliberative rather than rapid and intuitive.

4 *Proficient practitioners* are able to see situations holistically and identify the most important aspects of the case including recognising 'normal' and 'abnormal' patterns. A proficient practitioner has a wider range of routines and behaviours which can be brought to bear according to overall rules covering patterns.

5 *Experts* have developed a deep and intuitive grasp of situations and have a clear vision of what is possible and desirable in the longer term in a variety of circumstances. In taking decisions they do not rely on rules or conventions because they recognise and can respond to a wide range of patterns. They have an extensive repertoire of routines. They only have to employ analytic approaches in a limited number of instances. A further feature of experts is their ability to explicate and share their practice with others.

(adapted from Eraut 1994: 124)

Underpinning this model of development is the notion of a professional repertoire, similar to that of a musician, which describes the range of pieces he or she has learned to play. One of the things that characterises the development of expertise is the capacity to act with increasing flexibility, as you develop a wider range of skilled behaviours that you can bring to bear on your practice.

 Task: From novice to expert

Below is an extract from a recent review looking at the work of Chartered Teachers in Scotland. The respondents were asked to list some of the changes they noted in regard to their practice. What do you think this indicates about their level of practice – competent/proficient or expert?

Teachers' voices

'I have taken a problem-solving approach to my classroom practice. I've got greater self-confidence and I am much more prepared to experiment and try out new approaches.'

'I now see my subject as a vehicle for learning. If they're not enjoying something I'll respond by saying "OK, how do you think we should tackle it?" and going with the pupils' suggestions. Before, I'd have taken it as a personal affront.'

'I know what's trivia and what's the big picture. Before I was locked in my classroom practice but now I've got an overview and I know where all this fits and what matters and what doesn't.'

'I've got a lot more things in my tool kit and I'm more confident about switching and varying my approach. I'm more spontaneous in reacting to what's needed and what's going on. I'm more focused on learners. It's opened up a lot more possibilities so my classes now are much more active and alive.'

Whilst the novice to expert model is presented as an orderly succession of stages, we know that expertise is very dependent on context. All of us can find ourselves back in the role of novice if there is a substantial change to our professional context. You need to remember that if you are entering a new area of practice you may need to go back to forms of learning that you no longer find particularly useful in more established aspects of your practice. In reviewing your performance you may also find that you are at different 'levels' with regard to different aspects of your practice and this can therefore help you to identify what sorts of experiences will be most helpful to your development.

Professional standards

Most professions have established standards for professional practice which specify levels of performance for practitioners. These are used for a variety of purposes:

- training, development and qualification

- clarifying job expectations

- assessing performance

- self-evaluation and accountability.

The types of frameworks using professional standards are much more specific and detailed than the other two models we have looked at. Furthermore, they may be underpinned by a variety of models of practice, including elements of the two we have already considered.

Initially standards were introduced to make a clear separation between those who were qualified to practise and those who were not. However, this notion of an initial training being a licence to practise indefinitely is changing. In many fields continuous professional development is a central feature and where once there was a single standard for entry to the profession there are now several. For instance, in England the Standards continuum now encompasses:

- Qualified Teacher Status (QTS)

- teachers on the main scale

- teachers on the upper pay scale (Post Threshold Teachers)

- Excellent teachers

- Advanced Skills teachers.

(Department for Children, Schools and Families, 2007)

In Scotland one of the first standards to be developed was for headship, followed by a number of standards for teaching:

- an initial teaching qualification standard

- a standard for full registration as a teacher

- a standard for Chartered (accomplished) teacher.

Underpinning this series of standards is the idea that, by defining levels of performance, these standards represent a progression in terms of becoming an increasingly effective practitioner in a given field. Besides such vertical suites of standards we also have a proliferation of standards that represent different specialisms. In teaching, for instance in England and Wales, there are standards for teachers specialising in special educational needs and for teacher managers. Thus professional standards can represent two forms of career trajectory: one based on progression from novice to expert and another based on increased specialisation. Standards may be derived in a variety of ways. Some are based on behaviourist models of practice. These entail a functional analysis that involves recording and specifying the observable behaviours of practitioners. Others may be based on more holistic models that take account of both behavioural and cognitive elements of practice. Two extracts are presented in the Boxes.

Type 1: Core Professional Standards for Teachers (post-qualification level)

Professional standards are statements of a teacher's:

- professional attributes,
- professional knowledge and understanding, and
- professional skills.

They provide clarity of the expectations at each career stage. The standards clarify the professional characteristics that a teacher should be expected to maintain and to build on at their current career stage. After the induction year, therefore, teachers would be expected to continue to meet the core standards and to broaden and deepen their professional attributes, knowledge, understanding and skills in that context. There are 41 core standards, of which 9 define attributes, 16 define knowledge and 16 define skills. (Training and Development Agency for Schools, 2007)

Type 2: The Standard for Chartered Teacher (advanced or expert level)

There are four key components to the Standard for Chartered Teacher:

- Professional values and personal commitments
- Professional knowledge and understanding
- Professional and personal attributes
- Professional actions.

The basic assumption is that the Chartered Teacher is characterised by four central values and personal commitments:

- effectiveness in promoting learning in the classroom,
- critical self-evaluation and development,
- collaboration and influence, and
- educational and social values

and that these values and commitments are evident in nine types of professional action which, in their different ways, draw on professional knowledge and understanding of various kinds and a wide range of professional and personal attributes. (Scottish Executive, 2004)

 Task: Looking at professional standards

You have been given extracts from two professional standards. Both extracts are taken from the introductions to these documents.

- What are the similarities and differences between the two?
- What type of model of practice do you think each one exemplifies?

Working with standards

The professional standards that are specific to your area of practice will be central to organising and presenting the contents of your portfolio because these professional standards are the official, formally agreed framework for assessing progress and identifying learning needs.

You can use standards as a basis for both evaluating what you have learned so far and as a basis for identifying the capabilities that you need to develop. Look, for instance, at part of an instrument (Figure 2.2) that was developed in relation to a section of a standard for headteachers. This section of the standard specifies the professional abilities of a headteacher and it has been turned into a questionnaire that can be used for self-evaluation or adapted to gain feedback from others about how they perceive a person's performance. Figure 2.2 shows what this looks like for three of the specified abilities.

Advantages and disadvantages of professional standards

Standards have a number of advantages, particularly because they can be an aid to communication by making it clear to practitioners and other stakeholders what the profession is about and clarifying expectations. In this sense they remove some of the 'mystery' from professional performance and make it more open and transparent. This is particularly helpful when you are entering a field that is new to you. They also help to ensure that particular groups are not excluded from career advancement. Standards are publicly agreed criteria and advancement is based on meeting these rather than on patronage and having the right connections.

The disadvantages of standards

- *Fragmentation:* standards can fragment practice and divide it into segments in a way that may be helpful for novices and beginners but, because of the nature of professional practice, is counterproductive for developing proficiency and expertise. This is exacerbated in behaviourist models because the moral and cognitive elements of practice have been excluded, in which case they provide a restricted model of practice for novices as well.

- *Number of standards:* standards have a tendency to proliferate, partly because of a pressure for 'tighter' accountability but also the general tendency for the development of an increasing number of specialisms in many professional fields. In this way they can increase the compartmentalism of practice.

- *Demand for uniformity:* at a more personal level, in attempting to shape your experience to comply with a standard you may feel you are being forced to fit what you know and can do into a mould that feels contrived and artificial.

Nevertheless, where standards exist they are the accepted formulation for practice in a given field and can be used to plan your learning and build your portfolio based upon them. If you are working towards professional qualifications the relevant standard needs to be the backbone of your personal learning programme to ensure that you meet the prescribed criteria for successful assessment.

Figure 2.2   Professional abilities (*Source:* Scottish Qualification for Headship Western Consortium Course Material, 2001)

Interprofessional abilities	4	3	2	1	Comments
3.1.1 Demonstrates confidence and courage					
Is self-aware					
Manages self effectively					
Confident					
Is able to cope with ambiguity					
Able to confront difficult issues					
Deals positively with criticism					
Assertive					
Calm in a crisis					
3.1.2 Creates and maintains a positive atmosphere					
Is consistent					
Accentuates the positive					
Gives praise and encouragement					
Is optimistic					
Has good presentation skills					
Defuses potential problems					
Negotiates and handles conflict					
3.1.3 Inspires and motivates others					
Is supportive, encouraging, interested, committed, enthusiastic					
Well informed					
Responsive to others' needs					
Has a sense of humour					
Encourages creativity and participation					
Actively builds the confidence and capacities of pupils and staff					

 Task: Looking at a standard or competence framework

Select a standard that applies to your role. What aspects of your practice could you highlight to illustrate meeting different elements of this standard?

Summary: Exploring professional learning

In this chapter we have explored what it means to be a professional and we have delineated a number of models you can use to identify both what you have learned and what might be areas of further development for you.

Model I

The three elements model of practice

- Know why

- Know what

- Know how

This model is useful in giving you a simple and flexible formula for examining your practice in some detail and looking at how well the three elements of practice are matched together in your actions and in your plans for development.

Model 2

The novice to expert continuum

Novice → Advanced Beginner → Competent → Proficient → Expert

This model allows you to consider your development in very broad terms. It also alerts you to the need to consider different forms of learning experience at each of the stages of your development. In the earlier stages this will need a higher proportion of technical input (know what) and at the later stages more interactive support involving professional dialogue and discussion and the consideration of problematic cases (knowing why).

Model 3

Professional standards

Professional standards will be particular to your area of practice. A specific standard may also be the basis on which your portfolio will be assessed if you are using it to gain an award that has professional recognition.

3

Writing a Professional Autobiography

In this chapter we explore the idea of a professional autobiography and its place in the process of self-evaluation and planning of professional development.

Key ideas

- What is a professional autobiography?
- Reviewing and evaluating learning
- Career stages: from novice to accomplished practitioner
- Preparing a career timeline
- Mapping out significant experiences
- Planning a professional autobiography

Self-evaluation and professional learning

A portfolio is a demonstration of your learning as a professional, and in the last chapter we looked at ways of examining the process of your professional learning. In this chapter we will consider how, by writing a professional autobiography, you can begin to examine critically and in detail your own professional learning over a lengthy period. The purpose of a professional portfolio is to demonstrate the quality of your practice and your development as an educational practitioner and so a rigorous self-evaluation is the first step in the design and construction of your portfolio.

There are many ways to self-evaluate, with some approaches more extensive than others. Using a professional standard or a set of quality indicators is one way. A standard, competence framework or quality assurance scheme can each provide a set of criteria against which you can either rate yourself or write short evaluatory comments. We explored the use of professional standards as self-evaluation tools in the previous chapter. In this chapter we will look at a different approach to self-evaluation, using a narrative approach to 'take stock' in your career and to consider your future development.

Narratives of different lengths can be generated: a short vignette or account of a specific episode or situation, or a longer exploration of a clearly delineated set of experiences such as working in a particular role, or a full professional autobiography. A professional autobiography is a comprehensive review of your career as an educational practitioner and may also include other experiences, such as being a learner or working in another occupation. In a professional autobiography you as an educational practitioner can examine critically your development over the course of your career. In this chapter we will explore ways in which you can plan and write your professional autobiography and use this process as a means of self-evaluation.

A professional autobiography

A professional autobiography can be a very detailed exploration of your development over the course of your career. A professional autobiography can also be a more concise account in which you plot out those significant aspects – 'tipping points' – which have contributed to your development as an educational practitioner. Whether you write an extended autobiography in continuous prose or a more concise examination of your experiences and development, the objective of using a narrative form is self-evaluation and reflection. An important aspect of a professional autobiography is the idea of 'looking back to go forward', so in essence a professional autobiography is a summative evaluation of your progress to date with a view to determining the next stage of your development as an educational practitioner.

Writing a professional autobiography helps you to identify your strengths and to consider how you want to develop as a practitioner, this might be to:

- enhance your practice in a specific area

- deepen your understanding

- seek promotion

- move into another area or sector of education

- develop a specialism

- share your practice as an accomplished practitioner with novice practitioners

- lead a project group

- act as a mentor.

You may also have a more immediate purpose, of seeking accreditation of prior experiential learning (APEL). There are many programmes of professional development for teachers and leaders in various sectors of education where claims for credit can be made on what you have learned from the wealth of your professional experiences within your own work context. This process of writing a professional autobiography provides material to make a claim for the accreditation of prior learning towards a professional qualification or academic award. In this chapter we will look at how you plan and write a professional autobiography.

Writing an 'autobiography' might seem to be something that is very different from the professional development activities educational professionals typically complete. We tend to make a distinction between our personal lives and our professional lives, our feelings and our professional skills and competences. We usually associate 'autobiography' with the story of a person's life – often someone in the public eye, whether it is through their achievements in politics, sport, the arts or even notoriety, and this seems very different from the process of professional learning. However, we are increasingly aware of the importance of identity in the process of professional formation and development, and the writing of a professional autobiography is a useful way of exploring your awareness of yourself as an educational practitioner.

Experienced educators pursuing a Doctorate in Education undertake a professional autobiography as their first assessed task. The participants in this programme have reported that, initially, this is daunting. Trying to 'make sense' of a range of diverse experiences is a challenging task but nevertheless one that they find worthwhile. Typically the comments about the writing of a professional autobiography indicate that this task helped participants to:

- become more reflective

- have a clearer understanding of what they see as important

- have a sense of their own position – 'who I am as an educator'

- be better equipped to present ideas

- see what they have gained from their experience

- develop ownership and a sense of direction in their career.

 Task: The benefits of a professional autobiography

What would you hope to gain from writing a professional autobiography? Write down three or four ideas.

Who should write a professional autobiography?

A professional autobiography is often included as an activity in professional development programmes for experienced practitioners who will have considerable expertise and a wealth of experiences to draw upon as they explore who they are as an educator. A professional autobiography is not simply 'the story of my career' but a rigorous analysis of significant experiences and learning with the intention of planning further development. A professional autobiography is, therefore, a powerful tool for experienced practitioners to examine what they have learned during their career, to determine where their expertise lies and to consider how they might go forward. A professional autobiography can also help you take a 'helicopter' view not just of your own experience but how your experiences fit with current developments in your educational context and with wider educational trends and policies.

If you are relatively new to the education profession, a professional autobiography is also a useful tool for self-evaluation at an earlier stage in your career. Here you can use a professional autobiography as a way of reviewing your experiences as a learner and as a practitioner. Common threads between these two sets of experiences as well as some of the interesting contrasts that emerge will add to the process of self-evaluation.

Career-long development of an educational practitioner is now regarded as a vital element of what it means to be a professional. It is recognised that during the course of their career professionals move across a number of different stages. We looked at the idea of the development of a professional through a series of stages from novice to expert in Chapter 2. As an educational professional becomes more experienced, there are opportunities to acquire greater expertise, perhaps particular areas of specialism or to move into different types of roles: teaching, management, advisory, administrative, academic. Some practitioners may have very many different roles, each of which has the potential to be a rich learning experience in the acquisition of skills and insights. Other practitioners may have worked predominantly in one role, for example, as a classroom practitioner or an advisory teacher, or as a middle manager. In each of these instances, the educational practitioner has an in-depth experience with many opportunities to deepen skill and understanding, become more innovative and ready to take risks, knowing they are secure in their expertise. Whichever is your career trajectory, a professional autobiography is a way to consider how this wealth of experiences has made you the educational practitioner you are today.

Creating a timeline

A timeline gives you a broad framework to look at the overall trajectory of your career and helps you to begin to consider some of the highlights in your development as an educational practitioner. We will use some examples of ways of constructing a timeline. These examples of timelines are for three educational practitioners who have followed very different career trajectories.

 Task: Comparing timelines

Compare and contrast the timeline examples and identify any similarities and differences. How do these match with your own development as an educational practitioner?

Review of timelines

In Figure 3.1 we have the timeline of the career of an experienced primary teacher. Looking back over a career, it is sometimes difficult to recall when specific events occurred. Instead it is useful to work in broad blocks of time. This timeline starts with the teacher's first appointment and charts the different contexts where she has worked as well as the range of professional development opportunities that have had an impact on her as an educational practitioner. As you can see this timeline is not an exhaustive account of the teacher's career but maps out the key points. The process of creating a timeline enables you to set out these key areas in sequence. This teacher has only worked in two primary schools. Nevertheless, one aspect that becomes immediately clear is the wide variety of activities and professional development opportunities that this teacher has engaged in. Also, during a career break this teacher had other opportunities that she feels have added to her development as an educational practitioner.

The next timeline, Figure 3.2, is the shorter career span of an educational practitioner working in early childhood education. In contrast to the first example, this educational practitioner has worked in a wide variety of roles. Included in this timeline are the different posts he has held over the 10-year period of his career and some of the in-service activities he has undertaken.

Figure 3.3, the third timeline, is of a secondary school teacher working with children with specific learning needs who has been involved in a number of different curriculum developments projects. She has used these to pinpoint some of the important phases of her career. This teacher has also included her experiences as a pupil and student in her timeline because she felt these were significant to her development as an educational practitioner.

From these examples we can see that there are different ways of mapping out the trajectory of your career. A timeline can be based on:

- regular time intervals, for example, one year, two years or five years

- changes in posts

- changes in remits and areas of responsibility

- professional development opportunities

- school or curriculum development projects.

The timeline can also include areas beyond your professional life that have been important in your development as an educational practitioner. Your experiences as

 Task: A career timeline

Draw a timeline mapping out your career as an educational practitioner.

Figure 3.1   Timeline 1

Years	1–3	4–6	6–10	10–15	15–16	17–19	20–23
Role	1st post St Martin's Junior School	'Real Books' Project	Career break – 2 children; voluntary work in charity shop	Worked as a fundraiser	Returned to teaching

Maths Co-ordinator | Networked learning community | Gifted and talented inservice programme – school co-ordinator |

Figure 3.2   Timeline 2

Year	1	2	3	4	5	6	7–8	9	10
Activities	1st post Woodend Nursery School	Course on Child Development, OU	Literacy Co-ordinator	Move to Ellswood Nursery	Co-ordinator for 3–4 curriculum	Continued work on curriculum on LEA Working Group	Staff tutor – LEA for literacy in early years	Depute head at Stonebrook Primary	Begin headship qualification

Figure 3.3   Timeline 3

Year	Secondary school	University	Induction	2–4	5–7	8–10	11–12	13–16
Important aspect	Enjoyed school – thinking about teaching	Changed from English to Psychology and History	History teacher, Johnstown Secondary	Completed PG course on SEN	Move to SEN Unit	Pastoral Leader	Outdoor Education programme for Lower School	LEA Project – ICT & SEN

a learner or in other occupations or through personal interests which may have helped develop your skill or understanding of education and your role as an educator, might also form a substantial part of your timeline. Use these examples as a starting point to draw a timeline for your career.

In drawing your career timeline consider the following questions:

- What is the starting point?

- What are the different contexts you have worked in?

- What are the different tasks you have undertaken?

- What are some of the different developments you have been involved in?

- Are there any other experiences you might include?

Looking at significant events and issues

The career timeline provides an outline in which you can pinpoint specific events or experiences but it does not provide the detail of why these items might be important in your development as an educational practitioner. In addition, often because we are caught up in the immediacy of life in a classroom, college or early childhood establishment, we do not realise our development over a period. We need to be able to consider what has been significant in our development in greater depth:

- What insights, understandings and skills have you acquired from your day-to-day experiences?

- Why have some experiences or activities been more remarkable than others in your development?

- What have been some of the wider influences that have shaped what you have been involved in as an educational practitioner?

These questions help you to consider a more fundamental issue that is vital to your development as an educational practitioner: what kind of educator do you see yourself to be? This question brings us back to some of the ideas that we discussed in Chapter 2 about what it means to be a professional but we can extend this by considering what kind of educator you see yourself to be.

What kind of teacher or educational practitioner you see yourself to be is vital if you are to be able to have a genuine sense of ownership in reviewing and planning your development as a professional. The kind of educator you see yourself to be is also a core issue explored in the process of writing a professional autobiography. Expertise and the development of highly accomplished professional practice as an educator is not just a matter of acquiring additional skills or being able to perform the tasks in a more rapid, less conscious manner. At the heart of professional development is self-perception: how the teacher or educator perceives him- or herself and what he or she aspires to be as an educator. There is considerable debate about the limiting effects of the level of accountability and scrutiny educators are placed under in today's education system. Ball (2003) argues vigorously against the narrowing of the definition of what it means to be a teacher that has come about as a result of a target-driven policy agenda in education. However, there are other ideas about what it means to be an educator. Sachs (2003) argues for 'the activist teacher' while Forde and her colleagues (2006) argue for the development of teacher agency and the idea of the 'engaged professional'. An important aspect of agency is for an educational practitioner to be able to articulate who they are professionally and what they stand for in their professional lives. An extended professional autobiography is not just an account of your career or progress as an educator but is an exploration of your development against a wider backdrop.

Contexts for development

A professional autobiography can be a full account of your development and this can be a very demanding task in which you have to recall some of the detail of your progress during your career. However, a professional autobiography also enables you to ask more powerful questions about what you have learned from these different experiences. The next step then in developing a professional autobiography is to think about what has been significant in your development as an educational practitioner. Your progress as an educational practitioner is shaped by a number of factors:

- the different roles and responsibilities you have had

- the different educational establishments you have worked in

- the wider social and political contexts.

A professional autobiography enables you to position your professional formation in this wider frame. Your can consider your progress as an educational practitioner in terms of three spheres: self, organisation and social.

Self

An important aspect of developing your professional autobiography is your personal growth as an educational practitioner. Here we can consider your growing skill in teaching and your deepening understanding of the principles and theories underpinning your practice. There is also another aspect, that of the development of your identity as an educational practitioner: how you see and feel about yourself as an educator. Your own experiences as a learner, whether this is as a student in tertiary education or as a pupil in school, can also have a significant influence on your development. Here you can consider:

- your own experiences as a learner

- your own professional development

- the range of your activities and responsibilities as an educator

- family and wider social experiences.

 Task: Your experiences

Jot down some ideas relating to your own experiences as a learner and an educational practitioner and reflect on how these have influenced your development as an educator.

Organisation

All educational practitioners work within an organisational context. This might be a large metropolitan college or university or a small rural primary school or it might be a dedicated unit within a larger organisation or a community-based facility. Whatever the context you work in, it will have a profound effect on you as an educator, providing you with opportunities to practise and develop in specific areas. It may also limit opportunities in other directions. The organisation will have priorities, policies, guidelines and a culture that shape your practice and that of other staff members with whom you work and again these factors will take your development in specific directions. In your professional autobiography you can consider:

- contexts you have worked in

- colleagues you have worked with

- managers you have worked for

- staff you have managed and led

- students/pupils you have educated.

 Task: Organisational contexts

Jot down some ideas relating to your experiences in the different settings in which you have worked, the people you have worked with and the learners you have educated.

Social

The setting you work in, for example a school, college or in an early childhood unit, does not stand independently. The policies, practices and culture of the organisation will be influenced by government policy and wider social, economic and political trends. Issues such as increased social diversity in culture and lifestyle, economic changes, technological development and globalisation all shape what is expected of you as an educational practitioner. Here we can consider:

- social trends

- political ideologies

- technological changes

- media images and news reporting on education and social issues

- local and central government policy initiatives

- economic demands.

Task: Wider contexts

Look back over the period of your career and decide what have been some of the significant trends that have shaped your role as an educational practitioner.

Making sense of experiences

Janice Rippon (2005) in her study of teacher development devised a useful scheme to explore the factors that shape you as an educational practitioner. As she gathered the life histories of teachers she asked each to consider what were the significant events, people or personal feelings. These are useful dimensions to explore in planning a professional autobiography but as these dimensions all exist within a wider context, there is a fourth area to add, that of the socio-political context. These aspects will have shaped the choices you have made in your career in education (and possibly in other occupations), the development of your practice, your growing sense of yourself as an educator and the opportunities available to you. We will consider each of these dimensions:

- significant events

- significant people

- significant feelings

- significant wider contexts.

Significant events

Charting out the significant events in your career extends on the sequence of important points you mapped out in your timeline. These events might match stages in your development as a professional from novice to expert, or the structural stages within a teaching career such as the move from classroom practitioner to manager, or might be less formal. Nonetheless, these events are significant for your career progression. Such events might include specific tasks or experiences, for example taking responsibility for a school improvement priority, the first time you chaired a school meeting or led a CPD activity with your colleagues in school. Significant events might also include a specific professional learning experience that had a profound effect on your practice and how you see yourself as an educational practitioner.

Significant people

Significant people can include a range of people from within education and from other spheres of your life. There will be people you have met who have inspired you or encouraged you as an educational practitioner – these people may be in education themselves, might be family members or might be people from other spheres who have influenced your thinking about education. There may also be individuals who have not inspired you but instead have acted as negative role models. Even 'a negative role model' has potentially assisted in your development by helping you clarify what kind of educator you wish to be (and wish not to be!). Significant people might also include a particular pupil/student or group of pupils/students who are memorable in some way and from the experience of working with these learners you have grown as an educational practitioner.

Significant feelings

Significant feelings are not something that we tend to focus on when we look at the development of an educational practitioner's career. However, how you feel at a particular point in your career or in a specific context in which you have worked is a vital aspect in the process of making sense of your experiences. For example, think about the issue of your self-confidence: compare your feelings of confidence now to your feelings at the start of your career. If you take on a new role once again confidence becomes critical as you work to feel fully competent. What about your enjoyment of specific areas or the degree of stimulation or challenge you felt in a particular context? Perhaps you have been in situations where you felt little satisfaction in your work. How we feel often defines the value and potential of a situation or context for us.

Significant wider contexts

Wider contexts are important because, as we discussed earlier, education does not exist independently of other areas of society, particularly with the enormous range of central and local government policy in education and wider social, welfare and health areas. We have to take this wider context into account in any professional autobiography. You can consider the changes in education and other areas of social policy and the influence particular political or educational theories have had on what is expected of you as an educational practitioner over a period. These trends can have a profound effect on the kinds of areas and practices that are deemed appropriate or 'good practice'. Policies may have opened up different opportunities for you as an educational practitioner. For example, the growth in early childhood education may have provided you with opportunities for leadership. An emphasis on outdoor education or information technology may have provided you with opportunities to acquire new skills or take on new responsibilities. There is a further dimension of this wider context, that of the place of theory and research. As new ideas inform policy, these can shape practice and expectations.

We will use these four aspects – events, people, feeling and wider contexts – to draw up a more detailed plan for a professional autobiography based on the career timelines we discussed earlier.

 Task: Planning a professional autobiography

Review the example plans in Figures 3.4–3.6 and draw up a similar plan for your professional autobiography.

Figure 3.4 Plan 1

Years	1–3	4–6	6–10	10–15	15–16	17–19	20–23
Events	1st post St Martin's Junior School	Launch of project on using 'Real Books for Reading'	Career break – 2 children; voluntary work in charity shop	Partner's redundancy – get job as a fundraiser	Returned to teaching – part time Maths Co-ordinator	Networked learning community – working with teachers in other schools	Gifted and talented inservice programme – school co-ordinator
People	HT: traditional methods Stage partner – support	New HT College tutor	Husband & children	Supervisor – opportunities for training	HT – really there for the pupils	Some colleagues in network – exchange of ideas	Course lecturer – inspirational! Working with NQT
Feelings	Enjoyed working with pupils Frustrated – 'old methods'	Excited & challenged – understanding of chn's learning	At times bored & weary – part time job: not very confident	Learning to make decisions + teamwork	Very anxious, even 'real books' is a thing of the past Glad to be back	Difficult to deal with some in network – less committed & enthusiastic	Feel committed to G&T programme; enjoy working with NQT
Wider context	Demand for increased accountability	New ideas about emergent reading	Education on political agenda National Curriculum	Cutbacks – no full-time posts	UK falling behind on international scales – focus on literacy & numeracy: research on chn's writing/reading	Inclusion agenda – research on more able pupils – recent studies helpful Technological developments	Education and economic policy – high skills; achieving potential

Figure 3.5 Plan 2

Year	1	2	3	4	5	6	7–8	9	10
Events	1st post Woodend Nursery School	Course on Child Development, OU	Literacy Co-ordinator	Move to Ellswood Nursery	Co-ordinator for 3–4 curriculum	Joined LEA Working Group on Literacy in early years	Staff tutor – LEA for literacy in early years	Depute head at Stonebrook Primary	Start working towards headship qualification
People	Working with 4–5 year olds	HT very encouraging	Working with HT on literacy project	Very supportive staff & links with primary school		Working with different teachers and groups		SMT – really good ethos	Group on course
Feelings	Getting to grips with the job – fun! (at times)	Enjoyed course – good to have study and work side by side	New responsibilities – really enjoyed writing curriculum guidelines & materials	Younger children – more challenging but lots to develop	Management responsibilities – challenging but feel a buzz most days	Liked the variety – seeing different classrooms. Satisfaction of doing inservice – though very anxious at first!		Glad made the move to primary – feel have expertise in early years to offer	Group – same mind set and tutor asks hard questions; enjoying reading
Wider context	Economic policy and women's employment – Expansion of child care provision		Development in curriculum for early childhood – also attainment agenda and focus on early literacy; ideas about early intervention			Changes in teachers' career structures; new emphasis on leadership, effectiveness and accountability. Research on leadership in schools			

Figure 3.6 Plan 3

Period	Secondary school	University	Induction	2–4	5–7	8–10	11–12	13–16
Event	Small rural secondary – lots of opportunities	Changed from English to Psychology in 2nd year	History teacher, Johnstown Secondary	Completed PG Course on SEN	Move to SEN Unit	Outdoor Ed programme for Lower School	Pastoral Leader	LEA Project – ICT & SEN
People	Teachers, especially social subjects teacher	Holiday job as community worker	2 girls – 15 years old and switched off; hard to deal with – why am I doing this?	HoD for History – high expectations – opportunities to develop	Team leader distant but she was under pressure	Pupils on the Outdoor Education Programme	Pastoral team – and still the pupils!	Tutor on SEN/ICT – knows her stuff
Feelings	Enjoyed school – thinking about teaching	Enjoyed working with teenagers – can't decide teaching, Comm Ed maybe social work – which?	Hard work – feeling tired; worried not making an impact	More confident – still feel not reaching some pupils; SEN course really helps	Wow – but a challenge; pupils with multiple needs; trying to see the child not the problem	Made me think about what they can do – not what they can't do	Enjoyed the teamwork – didn't feel as isolated as I feared – real buzz at times	Frustrated at attitude of some staff – but admire commitment of majority
Wider contexts	Not really aware – glad to get to Uni	Community Ed under pressure no jobs	Accountability and league tables	Funding issues Technological advances SEN – using research from course.	Technological advances SEN – using research from course.	Inclusion agenda and increased spending on education: highlight life/employment skills		

In each of the plans there have been particular events that have been influential in the development of the educational practitioner but these events are a mixture of personal and professional: some are planned, some are more opportunistic. Further, the people seen as influential vary greatly – managers, fellow educators, learners, tutors – and there are even some negative role models. When we look at the significant feelings in these plans we can see that these are contextualised: an educational practitioner can be energised, de-motivated, feel they have no confidence, or inspired, and this is very much linked to the setting, events and people. What each grid also reveals is the importance of and the impact of educational and social policy and of research on what is expected of educational practitioners in their daily work.

Collaborating with others

A professional autobiography very much focuses on the individual practitioner. However, this does not necessarily need to be a solitary activity. There are many benefits to be derived from discussing your career development with others who have similar experiences or indeed who may have had very different experiences. The similarities and contrasts will help you to identify what have been some of your key developments. Further, your professional progress with a mentor or critical friend can help you develop a balanced self-evaluation. Often a critical friend will point to significant areas of achievement that you might not recognise. In Chapter 5 we look at different ways you can work with others to reflect and you can draw on these in the writing of your professional autobiography.

Summary: Planning a professional autobiography

In this chapter we have looked at planning a professional autobiography as a way of reflecting on your career and analysing your development as an educational practitioner. A professional autobiography is a powerful means of self-evaluation and reflection and can provide you with material to draw upon as you design and construct a professional portfolio.

We considered how to plan an autobiography by constructing a timeline that maps out the main events of your career in set blocks of time.

We also looked at different contexts for your development as an educational practitioner:

- self
- organisation
- social.

We examined a framework for making sense of your experience and progress as an educational practitioner by mapping out:

- significant events
- significant people

(Continued)

(Continued)

- significant feelings
- significant wider contexts.

For some professional portfolios you may be asked to produce a full professional autobiography whereas in others you may have to present a more concise self-evaluation or reflection. The strategies discussed in this chapter will help you to generate materials either for a full professional autobiography or a more focused self-evaluation. The self-evaluation is the first step in planning your learning, an area we will explore in the next chapter.

Action Learning

This chapter sets out to describe what action learning means in a professional context and why, as a holistic process of professional enquiry, it is particularly significant to your development and building your professional portfolio. It goes on to illustrate various types of action learning from the informal to the formal. Lastly it indicates how the evidence generated by action learning can help you to build your portfolio.

Key ideas

- **Action learning**
- **Professional enquiry**
- **Trial and error**
- **Action learning cycles**
- **Action research**
- **Project management**

Learning through action

Action learning is an important idea in the exploration of the development of professional practitioners. In using the expression 'action learning' we do not mean learning from such actions as attending a course or going on a visit to another establishment. What we mean here is *learning through taking professional action*, so this is a form of learning in which your own professional practice is the central vehicle for your learning. You learn through undertaking your work. Action learning is critical to the development of reflective practice and is the core of the material you present in a professional portfolio.

 Case Study: Questioning differently

Karen had a third year class (ages 14–15) who were not really engaging in her question and answer sessions at the end of the lesson. She was chatting with a colleague about it who mentioned something called 'wait time' as a technique for increasing the effectiveness of question and answer sessions. Karen decided she would like to try this out but she needed a little more information. She talked to a couple of teachers in the Science Department who had been using

(Continued)

(Continued)

the technique and got the chance to watch one of them in action. Karen soon realised it was not simply a change of technique she was looking at but also a change in her purpose for questioning her students. She read some of the material on cognitive acceleration as she began to work on developing her own questioning techniques and noting her students' responses. It took a while to get used to consistently using open-ended questions and letting students develop their answers. Having one of her colleagues observing and giving her feedback helped. With his support she gradually moved away from using questioning to check for retention to using it to develop the students' thinking about the lesson topic. She was pleased with the results – it seemed to her that her pupils were becoming more engaged.

In the Case Study example we can see a number of the different elements of action learning.

Projective and improvement-focused

Action learning is projective rather than reflective since central to action learning is imagining how things might be better. Action learning is based on a form of enquiry where what you are trying to find out is whether adopting *x* or *y* approach leads to better outcomes for your learners. It is experimental in the sense that you undertake a course of action in the belief that it will improve the quality of your practice. This means that you need to start with a hunch or a hypothesis that doing *x* or *y* will improve outcomes for your learners.

Values-driven

Going back to the model for practice that we proposed in Chapter 2, action learning is not a simple process because acting as a professional raises issues about your intentionality and judgement as well as matters of performance. Action learning is not a simulation, you are working with real learners so you have the obligation to try to improve outcomes for them throughout your engagement in action learning. Whilst you may be experimenting with new forms of practice you must do so responsibly and in the best interests of those you are working with. You are central to the action *as a practitioner* not as a non-participant researcher, or a scientist standing outside the context trying to preserve objectivity.

Identity-forming

Action learning can appear to be a purely technical matter of adopting a new approach or undertaking a new project. However, because you, in your professional role, are central to the practice of action learning it will also affect the nature of your professional identity to a greater or lesser extent depending on your focus for action. In that sense you will always emerge from action learning changed in some way and the change will be both personal and public because it occurs in the milieu of working with clients and others as part of practice.

Creative and inventive

Although there are established forms of good and effective practice in all professional fields, these are not transferred from one person to another in a simple form. For instance, a teacher needs to adapt and frame new ideas and techniques within his or her own context of practice to ensure it achieves maximum benefits for his or her learners. This is why there is always a need for experimentation, adjustment and adaptation to achieve the best fit of new ideas and techniques within your own particular context. In this sense you have to reinvent your practice as part of the change process.

Collaborative

Action learning is always collaborative in that it depends on working with pupils and students so it has to be considered in terms of an educator–learner partnership. However, the effects of action learning extend beyond this duality to affect all those involved in your context of practice so both colleagues and your organisation need to be party to any changes that you set out to make.

The chance to talk through and exchange ideas is a critical part of action learning for two reasons. First, developing understanding and clarity in relation to new practices is essential in judging when and how to use them, and secondly, because action learning always carries with it an element of risk and the likelihood that it will move you out of the comfort zone of your normal routine, it can be quite painful. Talking through what is happening helps you carry out the process of adaptation and supports you through difficult stages in the process of implementation.

 Task: Using action learning

Think about a time when you used an action learning strategy. Write out a brief description of what you did and what you learned from it. Did it share any or all of the features listed above?

Why action learning matters

Action learning is all about the improvement of your practice and it is based upon the notion of professional enquiry – an essential cycle of professional behaviour that underpins reflective practice. Professional enquiry is the means of learning how to learn as a professional practitioner because professional enquiry provides the means of integrating all the elements that go to make up practice.

Since professional practice is a complex mixture of values, knowledge, skills and judgement, changing and improving it requires that you learn through action. It is only through practice that you can begin to integrate and develop new elements and approaches into a form in which they become usable and sustainable as part of your professional repertoire. Action learning is critical to your professional development because it is the means by which, as a beginner, you develop your professional routines, and, as an established practitioner, it is the means by which you modify and develop the professional routines you have already established. It needs to be a key element of your personal learning plan.

Acquiring, adapting and establishing professional routines takes time (Day et al., 2007). In the 1980s Joyce and Showers (1988) undertook research into the impact of professional development on teachers and found it took, on average, 25 trials in the classroom with support and feedback before teachers were able to incorporate new practices into their working repertoires. So you need to allow yourself time to learn.

At a more reductionist level action learning is the activity that provides you with evidence for the effects of your growing levels of knowledge, understanding and competence on your own behaviour and on the outcomes of your practice. In particular, as it potentially generates evidence of practice, change and improved outcomes, it provides a vital source of data for your portfolio. We will now look at different forms of action learning.

Trial and error

Anytime we try out something new there is a necessary element of trial and error because learning a new action takes time. However, what may seem like a good idea when you watch an expert undertake it can be a very different matter when you try it out for yourself. Often you are presented with a finished article that may have taken years to develop. What you perhaps are not told about is how long it took for the person to develop the practice, the kind of problems they encountered and the details of what they learned about implementing it as part of their daily routine.

For instance, maybe you attend a course where you learn about an approach that has resulted in good outcomes for the presenter so you think you will give it a try. There are two problems with this scenario.

- Too often what is trialled is not really the practice in question because you have not had the opportunity to understand it well enough to carry it out.

- Without thinking through how this new approach might relate to your current pupils/clients and your working situation you do not really know exactly what you are attempting to improve and therefore how to adapt the new technique to your context of practice to make it effective.

Now this does not mean you should only experiment after long and detailed preparation but it does mean that adopting a rather more considered approach to change is likely to be more fruitful.

Action learning cycles

Action learning should be approached as a form of problem-solving and should start with something in your practice, or that of you and your colleagues, which you are not satisfied about. In other words, it should start with something that you feel you could improve. The next stage is to investigate exactly what the problems are because you do not want to spend time tackling the symptoms rather than the cause. For instance, the most obvious response to persistent disruptive behaviour by a class group may be disciplinary, whereas the cause of the misbehaviour might be a lack of engagement with the curriculum. The problem might be better improved by altering the way in which the pupils are expected to learn.

Once you begin to focus in on the nature of the problem you will start to get ideas about how you might tackle it, as well as new questions that you need to ask. The next stage is to find out something about what other people have discovered in relation to the issue by reading, talking to colleagues and, if the opportunity arises, visiting other colleagues/establishments who are reputed to be good at dealing with it. This will provide you with new ideas and help you to refine some of your own ideas. On the basis of this information and the knowledge of your own particular circumstances, you can make a plan of action. You can decide what you are going to try, what difference you hope it is going to make and how you can monitor whether or not it is working. You will also need to set a realistic timescale for seeing whether it makes a difference. In summary, a structured action learning cycle involves:

- Stage 1

  o identifying and investigating an issue
  o making a hypothesis about its most likely cause

- Stage 2

  o considering the ethical implications of intervention
  o deciding on what outcomes you hope to effect
  o choosing the action you are going to take
  o communicating with others about your intentions and securing engagement

- Stage 3

  o taking action and making the intervention
  o monitoring what happens
  o recording the results

- Stage 4

  o evaluating what you have learned
  o sustaining and communicating improvements in practice
  o identifying any issues that remain to be addressed

 Case Study: Getting started – Stages 1 and 2 in the action learning cycle

This case study illustrates the first two stages of an action learning cycle where a teacher is trying to develop creative writing with his class.

Improving the quality of pupils' writing is a priority in Evefield Primary School. Sean is particularly concerned about his pupils' creative writing, as is his stage partner. They take time to look in detail at the sort of work their pupils are producing and compare this with the performance criteria that are proposed for children at this age. Both of them decide to do a couple of observations in their

(Continued)

(Continued)

classes focusing on children that appear to be underachieving and to talk to them about what they think about writing lessons before they meet again. Sean also talked to the language co-ordinator and she passed him some material from the Assessment is for Learning initiative.

After comparing their observations and thinking about the ideas they had been given through the language co-ordinator, Sean and his stage partner decide that they want to see whether adopting a paired assessment strategy focusing on a couple of the criteria that relate to issues of content will help pupils to develop their written work. They decide they will try the new approach for six weeks and see whether it leads to any improvement in the children's work as well as in their enjoyment and enthusiasm for writing.

Both Sean and his stage partner explain the new approach to their classes and discuss how people are going to pair up and which criteria for assessment the classes should choose to help to develop their writing. They also report to the rest of the staff on their proposals for action and how the project is going.

 Task: Looking at monitoring

How would you suggest Sean and his stage partner go about monitoring what happens? What do you think would constitute good evidence of success?

Think of an issue in your practice that you would like to address. How might you set about investigating it in greater depth? Who and what would tell you more about the nature of the problem?

Looking at the monitoring of results from the intervention to develop creative writing is the third stage of an action learning cycle. In the fourth stage the outcomes are evaluated and then consideration is given to the next steps. This succession of events is summarised in Figure 4.1, which illustrates an action enquiry that followed two of these cycles.

Action research

Action research uses much the same cycle of events as structured action learning, in fact both methods trace their origin to Dewey's ideas of learning through enquiry (Lewin, 1952). Action research differs in that it incorporates the use of tools and activities that seek to make the process more rigorous both technically and critically and it is associated with a requirement to report publicly on the outcomes of the enquiry. Action research is something that practitioners usually engage in with the support of an external agency, in particular with Higher Education institutions, often as part of an accredited programme of continuing professional development and/or as participants in a specific development programme such as the project *Improving the Quality of Education for All* (Hopkins, 2002).

Engaging in supported action research will assist you to understand and access reliable methods of data collection, analysis and interpretation. It provides various tools for undertaking structured enquiries including:

Figure 4.1   One issue – two action learning cycles

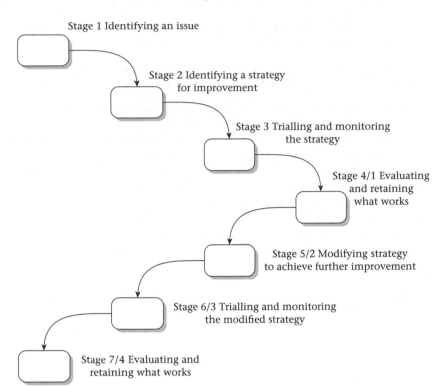

- guidelines on ethical practice

- observation schedules

- interviewing techniques

- documentary analysis

- using surveys and questionnaires

- interpreting performance data.

 Case Study: Monitoring and recording what happens – Stage 3 in the action learning cycle

Tanya is experimenting with the use of collaborative problem-solving as an approach to raise the attainment of her pupils in maths. During the first week of the intervention she takes some time to observe a sample of the five groups, taking short notes of what she observed. In one of the groups she notes that one of the boys in particular is not really engaged and that whilst one of the girls appears to be interested in the activity she does not actually say anything during the observation. The others hold a fairly rambling conversation as they try to apply one of the strategies they have learned to the problem. In reporting

(Continued)

(Continued)

back to the class the group presents a simple answer and they are not really able to explain much about how they tackled the problem.

As a result of her observations Tanya introduces some simple turn-taking techniques and ways of summarising and noting their ideas to the students.

A second observation three weeks later, again taking short notes of what she observed, showed that the group has now become much more engaged and confident in their working – the boy Tanya was concerned about is now joining in enthusiastically. She notes that the girl still does not engage much in the talk but on the one occasion when she does say something it is productive – '*Why don't we try …*' She notes that one of the group members does check that they have invited everyone's ideas. The presentation the group makes at the end of the session is much fuller than their first presentation and they are able to talk through the way in which their thinking developed.

 Task: Looking at practice

What do you think Tanya's notes tell her about the process of introducing collaborative problem-solving?

Has she acquired any evidence of outcomes in these notes?

Being involved in supported action research is likely to provide you with:

* access to previous studies and theoretical texts relating to your area of interest

* a more critically informed perspective with regard to professional practice

* an introduction to the discipline of reporting on empirical work.

Project management

If you are looking to develop your capabilities as a leader and manager then taking on responsibility for an improvement project within your organisation is a key means for both developing your own competences and for generating evidence of your learning. Such a project may be less clearly enquiry-based but, in essence, if it is about the implementation of practices that are supposed to improve the quality of provision for clients, then it should be. The management of the project should be centrally concerned with its impact on the learners in your school. All too often the temptation is simply to treat a development project as a task to be accomplished rather than as an exploration of the means of improving provision.

 Case Study: Taking on a whole-school project

Anusha, who has been a subject leader for a number of years, has taken on responsibility for the Leading Learning project in St Miles High School. Two teachers, one from social sciences and the other from the maths department, have been given temporary 23-month secondments for a day a week. Anusha's job is to work with them to develop and implement a two-year programme to introduce and embed collaborative learning in every department in the school. This will be the first time Anusha has taken on a whole-school responsibility and she is doing so both because she is very interested in the project and also because she feels she is ready to advance her career. She wants to use the project as a basis for demonstrating how she meets some of the criteria for the Standard for Headship.

This is a challenging project which will entail:

- team building

- developing the capability of the seconded teachers to work as change agents

- engaging and motivating staff from different subject areas

- developing cross-curricular structures

- focusing on changing classroom environments for learners

- building staff's capability to deliver collaborative learning

- using limited resources effectively.

Anusha needs to work with her new team, the staff and the Senior Management Team to clarify the aims of the project and formulate a set of objectives for the way ahead.

 Task: Areas of knowledge

What areas of knowledge do you think will be useful to Anusha in tackling this assignment?

What do you think will be the key abilities she will need to be able to carry it out successfully?

Evaluating the evidence from action learning – Stage 4 in the action learning cycle

As you undertake action learning there will be a great deal of information and evidence of your practice and the impact it has on learning. Providing you take care to collect data as you go, action learning will provide you with various forms of evidence that can be used to build your portfolio. Experimenting with your practice will also generate critical incidents. Recording these incidents and analysing what they reveal will form a basis for tracking and describing your own learning journey, as we illustrated in the case study on pages 47–48.

Action learning will also generate evidence about changes in practice and people's responses to the changes, including your own. Figure 4.2 maps out the way evidence for both the process and the outcomes are important. During your initial exploration of the issue you set out to address, Stages 1 and 2, you will have tried to generate valid and reliable evidence for the state of affairs, or baseline for your enquiry, prior to making a substantive change in your approach. At Stage 5 you will look at the same range of data to compare it with the baseline you established to see if the

Figure 4.2   Evidence for action learning: linking outcomes and process

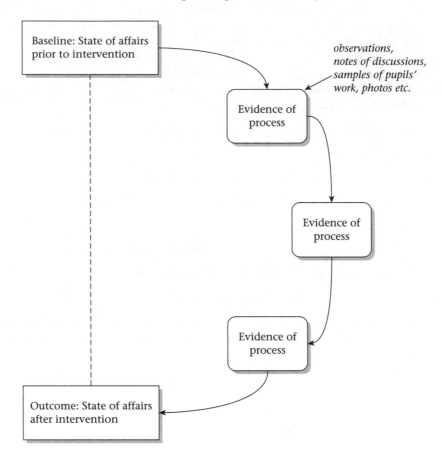

state of affairs has changed in any way. During Stage 3 you will be collecting on-going evidence that will enable you to describe the nature of the change process that you undertook and how people reacted to these changes.

These two sets of data will provide you with the basis for exploring the possible linkages between action and outcomes, as shown in Figure 4.2, which in its turn can serve as powerful evidence of your professional development and of your capabilities in your context of practice.

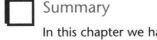 Summary

In this chapter we have looked at the characteristics of action learning as:

- projective and improvement-focused
- values-driven
- identity-forming
- creative and inventive
- collaborative.

We have also looked at the reasons why, as a process of professional enquiry, action learning is essential to developing your professional practice.

We have identified the various forms action learning can take:

- trial and error
- cycles of action enquiry
- action research
- project management.

The stages in the learning cycle are:

Stage 1

- Identifying and investigating an issue
- Making a hypothesis about its most likely cause

Stage 2

- Considering the ethical implications of intervention
- Deciding on what outcomes you hope to effect
- Choosing the action you are going to take
- Communicating with others about your intentions and securing engagement

Stage 3

- Taking action and making the intervention
- Monitoring what happens
- Recording the results

Stage 4

- Evaluating what you have learned
- Sustaining and communicating improvements in practice
- Identifying any issues that remain to be addressed

Lastly, we have looked at some of the kind of evidence that action learning can generate and how this can be used to build your portfolio, in particular your claims to display relevant professional capabilities and competences.

5

Reflection as Learning

In this chapter we explore the process of reflection and consider how reflection is an important aspect of professional learning. Here we will consider what is reflection and some of the key characteristics of the process of reflecting. We will also explore different ways of reflecting productively. Central to this discussion is the idea that reflection is a tool for advancing your professional knowledge and skills.

Key ideas

- **What is reflection?**
- **Reflection as a learning process**
- **Tools and techniques**
- **Using reflection to develop professional knowledge and skills**

In the previous chapter we looked at action learning as an important process in the development of your practice. In this chapter we consider the question of reflection as a means of promoting your professional learning. The notion of reflection as a facet of professional practice and as a means of enhancing practice is widely accepted. There is a considerable literature providing advice to teachers, nurses, doctors, engineers and other professionals on how to reflect more effectively. Much of this writing is concerned with the various strategies practitioners can adopt to reflect upon their practice. Here reflection is on and about action. Subsequent to the action or experience, the practitioner engages in a reflective process, whether through discussion or writing as a means of making sense of that experience. In this chapter we will set out, first, to answer the question of what is reflection? Secondly, we will identify some of the key characteristics of reflection as a process. Thirdly, we will consider some of the tools and techniques you can use to develop your ability to reflect productively on your experience. Finally, we will delineate the ways in which using reflection as a technique for learning will advance your professional knowledge and skills.

What is reflection?

Reflection is about making sense of our experience and thereby building knowledge and understanding of our practice. Reflecting means 'seeing again' but from a slightly different standpoint. Think of a reflection when we look in the mirror – we see our image in reverse – or when you see a mountain reflected in a lake it looks as though it is upside-down. Reflecting, then, gives us a different angle from which to view our experience. Normally it is an activity that follows on from experience. For most of us time to reflect on what is happening is not available in the midst of professional action.

Reflection is about looking back on what has happened to us and asking ourselves questions about it, such as:

- What was good in the lesson or unit of work?

- How might I improve on this?

- What was less successful?

- Why did it happen?

- What could I have done differently?

This questioning, in its turn, often generates new questions and ideas. For instance, there are things we might like to observe more carefully, or we might want to consider what the other people involved in the situation thought about it, or some new strategies that we might try out next time. In this way reflection through this questioning of our experience opens us up to new learning.

Reflection builds our knowledge. By drawing aspects of our experience to our attention and transforming that experience in thinking about it, we have insights we can apply to other situations. New questions will also be raised that we may need to pursue. Reflection alters experience. It can help us to codify and organise it. Reflection helps us to build it into patterns or schemas for analysing and developing our approach to problems in our context of practice. Reflection is a way of making sense of our professional lives.

Reflection can be something that happens almost by chance, in that we do it when something strikes us as odd or interesting in some way. Alternatively, it can be deliberately planned and structured because we already have in mind something we want to think about and understand. It can simply consist of ruminating about things from time to time or it can be part of a quite complex series of actions such as an action research project or a formal course of study using learning journals, action sets and/or coaching sessions to enhance professional learning.

 Task: Reflecting on an experience

Below, an art teacher is writing about her experience of setting up a collaborative professional enquiry project in her department. What has she learned by reflecting on her experience so far? What has she brought to her attention in terms of making sense of collaborating?

(Continued)

(Continued)

Teachers' voices   Working collaboratively

'I have found the experience so far to be in equal parts exhilarating and frustrating. As a teacher of a creative subject, the thrill of feeding off the ideas and contributions of my peers has been invigorating, as well as lessening the burden of the workload and the need to be inventive. Particularly with a creative subject there is a danger of a strong individual having undue influence. However a collaborative group helps to diffuse any "cult of personality", ensuring data is gathered and considered by a range of people. It was also important we had formed a united front on purpose and policy from the beginning so that no one person was able to dominate the direction of the project.'

'On a more selfish note I have found the experience of leading the group occasionally wearisome. Creative people often like to work alone and feel that taking ideas off others is a compromise. There have been some decisions made by the group that I would not have made myself. I have had to learn to accept these. An important part of reflection is recognising when your own opinions and views may be clouding your judgement.'

'Overall I have found that participating in the "community of practice" created by this collaboration has been very rewarding to me as a professional. It has made a welcome and productive change to the way we interact in the department.'

One of the disadvantages of reflection is that we are relying on our memory of events and this is often quite deficient. So, part of your professional learning is about improving your capacity to reflect in a more disciplined way that takes account of a wider range of evidence than is available to you if you just rely on remembering 'things' by chance.

Making reflection more effective

There are many ways of making your reflection more effective. First, you can make your questioning more systematic and rigorous in order to ensure you develop a more thorough understanding of any given situation:

- Exactly what happened, who did what and in what sequence?

- When did it happen and what were the consequences?

- How did the various people feel? What were the clues to their emotions?

- How did you feel?

- What are the likely long-term effects of what happened?

- Was it a good thing?

- Do you think what happened was just and equitable?

(Adapted from Tripp, 1993)

Task: Using questions to shape reflection

Look again at the comments made by the art teacher. Jot down which of the questions listed above the art teacher covers and which she leaves out in the extract.

Secondly, you can seek feedback from other people. You can ask your clients or students how they feel about the work that you are doing with them. What do they find useful, interesting or productive? What do they find less helpful? You can also ask your colleagues' opinions regarding particular scenarios and issues or invite their observations of your working practices. Thirdly, you can use tools and procdures to help you improve the efficiency of the reflective process.

These are three ways in which you can help yourself to become more attentive and observant when it comes to gauging what is significant about different situations as a basis for exercising your professional judgement. We will cover these in greater detail in the next section. Developing habits of reflection will help you to become much more self-aware and analytic with regard to your own professional actions and attitudes.

Stages in structured reflection

Stage 1

The first task is to *capture the moment* during the flow of action. This can be a difficult task because in the immediacy of the situation there will be a number of demands being made of you. However, there are some things you can do:

(a) *paying attention:* sometimes you pay attention because an incident strikes you as significant, at other times it may be that something you heard from a colleague or read in a journal that motivates you to look at a particular aspect of your practice in more detail;

(b) *making an initial record of your observations:* this can be very brief – simply a reminder that there is something you may want to reconsider later.

Stage 2

Then, preferably on the same day, when you have a little more time, you can *record significant features of the incident* to ensure you have a better description of what happened (you can use the first four questions listed in the previous section as an aide-mémoire). Once this is done you can return to interpret and evaluate the scenario some time later. This initial recording of the event may raise some other questions you would like to chase up. Perhaps you want to make another observation or find out what other people have written about the issue (collect and record more data) before you are ready to work through the implications that the incident raises.

Stage 3

You might also want to *check how your viewpoint compares* with those of the other people involved. You may want to seek their opinion about what happened and enter that into your record.

Stage 4

Once you have collected the data you are ready to start *interpreting and explaining* what happened and why you think the incident occurred (you can use the last three questions in the previous section here). You are ready to identify what the problems were and also to evaluate their significance.

Stage 5

Again you may want to *check how your interpretation compares* with colleagues', or find out whether anyone else has experienced similar issues from looking at some of the research literature.

Stage 6

Lastly you need to think about what the *implications of your analysis* are for your practice in the future. Do you want to change the situation and, if so, are you clear about why you want to do so? How do you think you might go about it?

Reading this list of activities it is clear that collaborating with others in the reflective process is very helpful. Talking things through with someone else will often help to clarify your thoughts and understandings.

 Task: Building your reflections

Think back to an incident in your practice that you can remember and try to analyse it using the questions on page 53.

Over the next week choose a particular incident to explore in greater depth using the stages in structured reflection as well as the questions.

Compare the results.

Another way of thinking about this more structured approach to reflection is as a process for developing the various intelligences you need to apply in making judgements about your work. These intelligences are about the nature of situations, people and yourself since these are the elements that go to make up your context of practice. Figure 5.1 shows intrapersonal, interpersonal and situational intelligence contributing to the three knowledges we identified as essential to professional practice in Chapter 2 on page 14.

Using tools for reflection: making the most of your experience

In this section we are going to consider five tools or techniques you can use to support your learning. The first three are tools you can use for capturing data and the final two will help you with the process of analysis. These tools are:

- learning journals, including audio/video diaries

- elicitation: using pictures and objects

Figure 5.1 Three key forms of intelligence

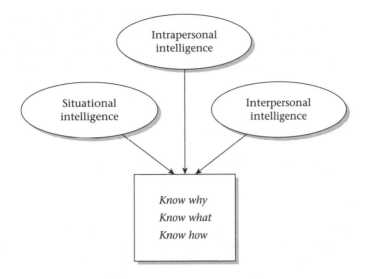

- audio/visual recording

- critical incident analysis

- co-coaching.

Learning journals, audio/video diaries

Keeping a learning journal or diary can be an important aid to your learning. If you look again at the stages in reflection that we outlined earlier you can see how keeping a dated record of observations, thoughts and feelings can help you to build and develop your capacity to make sense of your experience. A written journal has the advantage of being easy to re-use – if you leave space you can go back and write your reflections next to your original observations (a bit like double-entry book-keeping). You can use extracts from your journal as evidence of your learning in your portfolio.

Your learning journal can also serve as a point of collection for all types of data that you find useful – you can use drawings, diagrams and mind maps, you can inter-leave your written reflections with photographs or photocopies of material that you want to think about in relation to a particular incident or issue. If writing is not for you, an audio or a video diary may be the answer. An audio/visual recording of your initial impressions of an incident can work as well as a journal entry. Hearing and seeing yourself adds another dimension and can serve to remind you later about how you felt about things at the time of the recording.

A learning journal is a powerful tool to support reflection but it can be quite difficult to get started and to develop the habit of using it regularly. It helps to remember that it is *your* journal, so choose a booklet that you really like in terms of its size, feel and appearance and develop your own way of working with it. You can experiment with notes, drawings, inserts, Post-it notes etc. Whatever helps you best in thinking about and understanding your professional experiences is the right way to use your journal.

Elicitation – using pictures and objects

Sometimes it can be hard for us to express how we feel about things, even to ourselves. We may also find it difficult at times to begin to explore situations from a new position rather than relying on our usual way of thinking. Pictures and objects can sometimes be helpful in enabling us to do this. Choose an object or a picture to represent:

- how you feel about a situation

- what you feel about your current practice

- the way you see your students, pupils, course participants

- what you would want to be like as a professional.

Choosing an object may free you up to start thinking about these issues in ways that offer new insights and understandings about yourself and your development needs. The extract below illustrates this process and is taken from a conversation with a teacher who was asked to bring three objects to signify what had been the most important aspects of a course she had undertaken. This discussion formed part of an interview conducted for an evaluation study. In this extract one of the three objects – 'traffic light tins', an object used as part of assessment for learning – helps the teacher identify what mattered most to her about her course expectations as both a professional and a person.

 Teachers' voices: Using elicitation

'The reason I chose the wooden box was because it represented my teaching before. It was kind of very enclosed, and tight somehow. After being part of the project it's like the lid has been lifted and although I haven't had a chance to fully get out of it I'm now thinking differently. It has expanded the way I look at what I'm going to do in the classroom – I'm beginning to stretch myself again as a teacher.'

'I have chosen a sieve because I think what I feel I have learned is to distinguish between what's important and what's not. I still have a lot to learn – but I know what I'm looking for now when it comes to materials. I have a way of making much better decisions about what will suit my teaching aims.'

'The reason for choosing the Plasticine is that, as a professional, I've learned that you should never be closed off to new ideas. For instance, working with the group I've learned that you should be open to using new technology but you should have the confidence to know that you don't just take it off the shelf. You need to bend and shape it like the Plasticine until it works for you and your pupils. Actually it works both ways because it also represents the way I've had to bend and adapt as well – but that's OK. It's been good because that's what learning's about.'

Audio/visual recording

Where it is appropriate, and with the informed consent of those involved, audio/visual recording of professional practice can be a useful way of providing material for both discussion and reflection. The advantage is that things that you do not ordinarily see or hear – such as yourself in action – or to which you have not tended to pay attention in the past can be brought to the foreground for consideration. Obviously this can be a rather time-consuming exercise and will not be something you want to do frequently, but used at particular points in your development it can be very fruitful.

Taking a photograph can also serve to make a record of what happens. Like a note in a learning journal, it can serve as an aide-mémoire. You can also get others involved in selecting what should be recorded: *what pictures might students or pupils want to take to illustrate how they feel about the way they are being taught or treated?*

Critical incident analysis (CIA)

David Tripp (1993) provides a four-stage critical incident analysis for developing professional judgement:

- *Practical:* where the focus is on looking at the procedures involved in sets of incidents or episodes

- *Diagnostic:* where the focus is explaining the incident by looking at the causes, effects and meaning of the incident or episode

- *Reflective:* where the focus is on your personal response and evaluation of the incident or episode

- *Critical:* where the focus is on relating the incident or episode to wider issues of theory and the purposes of education.

The first stage involves practical judgement, which is the basis on which we decide what to do as we are actually engaged in practice. The other three forms of judgement – diagnostic, reflective and critical – all relate to reflecting on an incident after engaging in professional action. These three forms of judgement are hierarchically arranged and have a range of questions associated with each. The diagnostic stage is the most extensive, while reflective and critical judgement raise fewer questions because they depend upon a thorough diagnosis of what happened in the first instance. At each stage there are some typical questions we can consider.

Practical: at this stage, as you engage in the sets of practices, the questions Tripp (1993) suggests would focus on areas such as:

- *What should I do, how, when and where should I do it?*

Diagnostic: at this stage you are starting to look back at your practice after you have undertaken the professional action and initial typical questions relate to describing the incident or episode and considering the impact on those involved:

- *What happened, what were the causes of this incident?*

Also at this stage you are trying to understand the nature of the incident and why it might have happened, and so typical questions would be:

- *Why did this occur and what does this incident mean?*

Reflective: once you have been able to diagnose the incident and what it means you move on to the reflective stage where you begin to make some judgements. The perspective here is from your own position as a professional and you can consider whether this was an incident you felt comfortable with, whether it had a positive effect on all involved. Questions to ask at this stage include:

- *Am I comfortable with this situation, if so why, if not why?*

Critical: at the critical stage you relate the specific incident to wider concerns both to theory and to the principles and purposes of education. Thus at this stage you consider how a particular incident or episode relates to theoretical understandings. For example, there has been a critical incident in which you observed significant differences in the motivational levels between different groups of learners and so you can relate this incident to theoretical discussions about learning, differentiation and motivation. Another example might be as a leader you noted that there seemed to be conflict in a recently established team and you can seek to explain why this has occurred by relating the incident to theories about team development. In addition, you can relate your actions and decisions in this incident to wider ethical concerns about the purpose of education. The types of questions at this stage could include:

- *What is this incident an example of?*
- *Are the professional actions just and ethically sound?*

Tripp (1993), in his book *Critical Incidents in Teaching: Developing Professional Judgement*, will provide you with greater detail about this form of reflection. Critical incident analysis provides a framework for looking in detail at a particular segment of your experience. You can use it as a heuristic (a means of helping you discover what is significant) to guide your own reflection or you can collaborate with someone else and ask them to take you through the various stages of questioning. There are a number of possible outcomes of this process, including:

- a decision to undertake further exploration and analysis because it emerges that you do not yet have a full understanding of the situation

- a decision to explore certain approaches to improving the situation by searching the literature or undertaking a relevant course

- a commitment to try out a particular strategy which you think will address some of the issues.

Co-coaching – using structured conversations

Working with another educational practitioner is very helpful because you can act as sounding boards for each other, and give each other feedback based on observations of each other's practice. You may want to collaborate in an action learning project so that both of you are trying out the same approaches and you can reflect jointly on what you are learning. You can add to the effectiveness of this collaboration by choosing to act as coaches for one another. Co-coaching involves working together using structured conversations. In these conversations one person takes the role of the learner while the other person, acting as coach, assists the learner to reflect on his or her experience. The pair then reverse roles and the person who was learner acts as coach whilst the coach becomes the learner and the focus of the session.

Co-coaching is a way of developing critical professional dialogues with the aim of supporting professional growth. It is important to establish from the beginning the basis on which you are going to work together. You need to discuss and agree:

- levels of confidentiality

- how you will support and challenge each other's thinking

- your expectations of each other as both learner and coach.

You will also need to sort out the logistics of your working together, such as the purpose of your collaboration and how often and over what period you are going to meet. Effective co-coaching involves a structured professional dialogue, rooted in evidence from the learner's practice and context, which articulates existing beliefs and practices to enable reflection upon them.

A structured dialogue:

Step 1:   You need to agree the parameters of your relationship because if it is going to be of value both partners need to feel that they can be honest and open with each other. It is essential that you discuss what you think you each require as ground rules for establishing this sort of relationship and that you come to an agreement about what they will be that satisfies you both.

Step 2:   In co-coaching you need a structure for turn-taking in relation to two roles:

acting as coach – essentially listening to your partner, actively helping them:

- to clarify their experience

- to explore feelings and intentions

- to consider their values in action

- to explore the outcomes of professional action

- to identify their learning

- to identify next steps for their own development.

As coach, your task is to assist the learner to make sense of their experience and to identify ways in which they can improve their practice incrementally; in essence, you are supporting them in reflecting on practice as a basis for experimenting with new behaviours.

acting as a learner – essentially being open to explore issues relating to your practice:

- talking about your experience, your understanding, your professional values and beliefs, your feelings

- being prepared to examine all of the above in the light of evidence

- being prepared to actively engage in developing your practice.

As a learner, you cannot always know what you want to change or learn in relation to your practice at the beginning of the coaching process but you do need to be open to experimenting and trying out new behaviours.

A format for a structured dialogue

The person taking the learner role opens the session. You describe what it is that you want to consider and your colleague, as coach, simply listens. (After the initial session this will be about the outcomes of the action you agreed at the end of your previous session.) Once you have completed an initial account of the incident or issue the dialogue begins. The coach helps you to articulate the following stages:

- extending your **description** – clarifying things that were fuzzy, filling in gaps in your account

- **diagnosing** what the various parameters of the issue are: what, who, how, when, why

- **evaluating** the significance of what you have talked about, what has it to say in relation to your professional/educational values

- identifying **learning** – what are the implications for your development

- developing ideas for **action** between sessions – things you can do to build on your learning.

This process should take 20–30 minutes. You then reverse the roles.

Structured dialogues are not like ordinary conversations where you take turns to speak, so they may feel a bit strange at first. This is particularly so when you are in the coaching role because it largely involves listening rather than talking. Not only does this feel strange, learning not to add your own anecdotes and comments, but you will find listening actively is very hard work. However, it is worth persisting with the structure because it really helps to foster reflection and learning.

 Task: Using techniques for reflection

Try using at least two of the techniques. If you decide to use a learning journal you will need to do it for at least a couple of weeks to get a feel for the technique. Likewise with structured conversations, you need to hold a couple of sessions to realise the potential of this type of professional dialogue.

What were the benefits and drawbacks of using the tools you chose?

Outcomes of reflection

Reflection is not simply talking about or thinking about your past experiences and practice. It is essentially about developing your knowledge, understanding and skills as a practitioner. The core of reflection is professional learning. Therefore, we need to consider the outcomes of reflection.

Building your knowledge and understanding of contexts

In Chapter 2, when we looked at the Dreyfus and Dreyfus (1986) model for the development of professional performance from novice to expert, what marked the experts was that they had developed a holistic understanding of cases and contexts. Reflection helps you to build the kinds of schemas and frameworks that improve the quality of your professional judgements. People can have much the same experience but without reflection some of them may never develop their practice: *'Jim's had twenty years' experience – the same experience repeated twenty times'*. Reflection and case review are critical to your learning because they relate directly to the lived experience of practice in all its complexity and as a practitioner this is what you need to learn to make sense of.

Improving communication

Reflection is also a practice that, in its more structured form, enables you to combine theoretical and practical insights and develop a language for discussing and describing what you do. This will help you to develop your self-confidence as a practitioner and improve your capacity to communicate and account for your practice.

Developing self-awareness

As we claimed earlier, you are central to your practice and therefore it is important that you are aware of both your strengths and your limitations. Reflecting, particularly in relation to the feedback you are getting from others, is essential to developing self-awareness so that you can maximise your strengths and either address or minimise the effects of your limitations.

Developing your capacity to observe, collect and analyse data

Once you start the process of questioning your experience you will find that you become increasingly sensitised to your context. With an inclination to pay close attention to a wider range of data, your ability to observe and, with careful questioning, to make sense of what is happening, will increase with time.

Learning to see the bigger picture

Reflection will also help you begin to identify patterns and sequences and to become less tied up in the here and now and less distracted by disconnected details. As you begin to develop a more holistic overview it helps you to concentrate on what is important in the longer term. Your ability to prioritise and decide where to put your efforts will improve as a result.

Improving projection

Finally, it is important to remember that although reflection is about looking again at what has already happened, its real purpose is to provide us with guidance for the future. It needs to be associated with an imaginative leap into how things can be improved and how you can be an active agent in making a difference.

Reflection and the professional portfolio

An integral part of a professional portfolio is the reflection on your learning and development as a professional practitioner. However, reflection should also be a dynamic element of your practice, something you engage in regularly and for which you can use a variety of tools and approaches. Developing a structured approach will make reflection both a more effective learning experience as well as generating rich material that can be included in a portfolio. The range of techniques explored in this chapter will help you to create records of your reflection and your development over a period of time using different media, all of which are possible elements of a professional portfolio.

 Summary

Reflection is a vital aspect of professional learning and practice and you will often be asked to demonstrate your use of reflection in your portfolio. In this chapter we have looked at what reflection is and how it can be both an informal and a formal process.

We looked at three ways of making the process of reflecting more effective:

- patterns of questioning
- seeking feedback from others
- using tools to aid reflection.

We outlined the stages that are followed in the process of structured reflection:

- capturing the moment
- recording what happened
- checking our impressions with others
- interpreting and explaining the data
- checking our interpretation
- drawing out the implications for future practice.

We looked at five tools/techniques that you can use to aid reflection:

- learning journals (and/or audio/visual diaries)
- elicitation
- audio/visual recording

- critical incident analysis
- co-coaching.

Lastly, we looked at the learning outcomes of reflection and their relation to professional development:

- building knowledge and understanding of contexts of practice
- improving communication
- developing self-awareness
- developing your capacity to observe, collect and analyse data
- learning to see the bigger picture
- improving projection.

6

Recording Learning and Practice

In this chapter we focus on the question of providing evidence of professional development and learning. Two critical questions are explored: What is evidence of learning? and What makes good evidence? We also examine a variety of ways of gathering and recording evidence of learning.

Key ideas

- Evidencing practice
- Forms of evidence
- Ethics of evidence

An evidential approach to practice

An important aspect of the claim we make for ourselves to be professionals or in seeking professional recognition is that we must be able to substantiate and evidence such claims. It is no longer sufficient to have our professionalism recognised solely in the regard/esteem with which we might be held by our peers, managers and clients. Demonstrating competence and professionalism through a portfolio can provide independent verification of this and so legitimises claims for enhanced professionalism and practice.

Providing evidence in support of claims for competence and professionalism is a central component of a professional portfolio. This evidence should be carefully selected to best reflect and support the claim that is being made. Here we explore some of the strategies practitioners have found helpful in gathering evidence for their portfolio.

Getting started

Gathering and selecting evidence can seem like a daunting task initially. It is important to remember however that your portfolio should reflect your current practice. You are not being asked to generate new materials but to provide resources that are typical of your day-to-day work. This might be work in a classroom as a teacher, where you want to demonstrate your work in a particular area of the curriculum, or as a lecturer where you want to highlight a particular aspect of pedagogy such as the development of thinking skills. It might be your work as an aspiring school leader and illustrates your work in leading a specific subject area or a change project. Many educational practitioners sort and organise resources and materials at the beginning and end of term. This is a good time to evaluate resources and materials to consider whether they would be useful in a portfolio. Place selected items in a suitable file for storage, such as a box file. It is a good idea to date and label each resource when you place it in the file. You will be surprised at how quickly you are able to build your evidence base by adopting this approach.

Reminder:

- It is never too early to start evidence-gathering.

- Store selected evidence in a suitable format, e.g. a box file.

- Sort, date and label evidence as you go along.

What makes *good* evidence?

Good evidence will clearly show your learning and development. However, *good* evidence depends upon the quality of the accompanying commentary or annotation. It is not enough to simply include a piece of evidence in a portfolio. You must explain why this piece of evidence is important, what it illustrates and, if appropriate, how it relates to a professional standard or benchmarks.

A good question to ask yourself is 'What is this evidence indicative of?' Does it show a particular competence in ICT, for example. Or does it demonstrate how you have applied learning from a course to develop a learning resource? Or, if you are looking at the development of your role as a leader, does it illustrate some dimension of leadership, for example, the way you led a development team revising a school policy? It is crucial that such explanations are included in your commentary or annotation in a succinct and focused way.

Good evidence also needs to be carefully selected. The important task in preparing your portfolio is to decide what material to include. You should not include every item that has been generated in the course of the project(s) you will be basing your claim on, but include those materials that clearly illustrate your claim for competence in relation to the particular core activity and its associated tasks. You should also remember that you may only need one good example rather than several items that are not well matched. Do not pad out the portfolio with additional material you have put in for 'insurance purposes'. What is important is that the evidence you select illustrates the process you undertook in fulfilling the specific core activity.

For example, while it may be tempting to include a class set of worksheets you have designed, it is better to select a small number that best illustrate the point you are trying to make. If your aim is to demonstrate development, improvement and a change in practice then you may wish to include 'before' and 'after' examples. Similarly, you may have conducted an audit in several classrooms using a short questionnaire. Again, one or two illustrative examples and a summary sheet collating the results and identifying areas for action would provide useful evidence.

Task: Selecting evidence

Gather together a small selection of evidence and then review each item deciding whether/how it could be usefully included in a portfolio.

In making a selection of evidence it is important to remember that:

- one item of evidence can illustrate a number of activities

- all items should be dated

- all items must be made anonymous.

Figure 6.1 shows the generally accepted criteria for selecting evidence to include in a portfolio. We look at each in a little more detail below. You may find it helpful to use these as a checklist when selecting your evidence for your own portfolio.

Figure 6.1 Evidence selection criteria

Relevance   Is it directly related to the claims being made in the portfolio?

Sufficiency   Is it adequate in quality, volume and range to fully reflect the claims being made in the portfolio?

Authenticity   Have you been directly involved and is your contribution capable of independent verification?

Currency   Is it reflective of current practice?

Competence   Were the intended outcomes achieved through effective and ethically sound practice?

Relevant

The evidence provided should be *relevant*, that is, directly related to the claims being made in the portfolio, both in terms of content and chronology. For example, if one of the pieces of evidence you are thinking about including in a portfolio is a set of minutes from a meeting, then you need to consider whether the matter was actually discussed at the meeting (which the minutes should record) and whether the date of the meeting (also recorded in the minutes) corresponds generally to the time frame indicated in your commentary. Is the evidence directly linked and related to the critical commentary in the portfolio?

Sufficient

The evidence is *sufficient* if it is adequate in quality, quantity and range to clearly exemplify the claims you are making in the portfolio. We have already noted the importance of 'good' evidence above. The volume of evidence included in a professional portfolio depends very much on the individual, since professional experiences and development can be so widely varied. However, an approximate guide might be an A4 lever arch file, A4 box file or 15–20 webpages if using an electronic portfolio.

An important element in ensuring that evidence is sufficient is to check that a 'range' of evidence is included, in other words a variety of pieces of evidence. This will provide a fuller illustration of the claim being made and also serve to authenticate the evidence. The range of evidence that might be included in a portfolio is discussed below.

Authentic

The evidence should be *authentic*. The evidence you include should reflect your own work or work that you have contributed to. If the latter, your contribution in relation to that of others should be clearly stated and if possible quantified. For example, you may have been a member of a school working party responsible for developing school policy on health promotion. If you include the final policy document as evidence, you should indicate the extent of your involvement in your commentary/annotation. If you were the leader of the working party, clearly your involvement and contribution would have been greater than other members of the group and this should be reflected in the commentary. The evidence you include should be capable of independent verification, which is one of the advantages of including a range of evidence. This can be captured through testimonials and witness statements. Care needs to be taken when seeking testimonials and witnesses statements, particularly if they involve pupils or parents. While it may be acceptable to provide a template for these, dictating or directing their contents is not, and rather than enhancing authenticity can sometimes compromise it. The ethical issues associated with providing evidence in a portfolio are discussed later in this chapter. Providing a range of evidence that includes independent verification is an important way of showing that the evidence is reliable and valid.

Current

The evidence provided in a portfolio should reflect *current* practice, generally within the past three years, often no more than five years and only exceptionally more than five. Evidence from previous years may be useful in demonstrating development, improvement and change in practice and so offer a comparison with current practice.

Competent

The evidence should demonstrate *competent*, i.e. effective and ethically sound, practice that achieves successful outcomes, evidenced through monitoring and evaluation.

 Task: Evaluating evidence

Go back to your selection of evidence and review each item using the criteria listed above.

What constitutes evidence?

Education practitioners will have a broad range of evidence to choose from to include in a portfolio. This can be *direct* and *indirect* evidence and *independent* evidence. In this section we consider possible sources of evidence that could be included in a portfolio.

Direct evidence

Direct evidence consists typically of documents, materials, resources or artefacts that were produced as part of the work about which you are writing: for example, an organisational development plan, a conference you organised, a statement of standard procedures in your workplace, an induction programme or a report. When including these you should illustrate:

• what you have done

• what others have done as a result of your project

• the outcomes/results of this work – whether this is in terms of change in practice or the outcomes achieved by the learners.

Indirect evidence

Indirect evidence is generally materials that comment on or testify to your carrying out of specific activities within the projects that form part of your claim. They might simply be the practitioner's own demonstration (in what he or she is now writing) of the knowledge or skills he or she claims to have acquired. It might also be something like a testimonial from a colleague or from a line manager. Such referees' reports could be briefly summarised in the main text and presented in full as appendices.

Figure 6.2 Types of evidence

Direct evidence	Indirect evidence
• agendas and minutes • procedures • draft and final policies • code of practice • discussion papers • staff development materials • guidelines • starter papers • plans and reviews • audits • questionnaires • interview evidence • position papers • letters and memos • evaluation materials • monitoring evidence	• ongoing review notes • diary • critical incidents log • learning journal • observations of your activities • (e.g. observations of your conduct of meetings) • witness statements

Independent evidence

Independent evidence consists of materials produced by someone other than the practitioner who is making the claim. These could be materials produced by pupils or students, letters from parents, views of colleagues, assessments by line managers and conclusions from outside specialists and so on. Accreditation of Prior Learning (APL) claims should always have an appropriate amount of independent evidence, sufficient to assure an assessor that the claims being made are supported by other people. (It will not be possible to have independent evidence for every single competence or benchmark but equally a claim based solely on your perspective as the claimant may have limited credibility.) A *witness testimony* is one way of providing indirect but independent evidence as part of a claim for professional competence.

Witness testimony

A witness testimony is a form of evidence that illustrates the conduct and/or completion of a particular project or task. Generally, witness evidence should be combined with other corroborative evidence, including evidence of training, development of knowledge and understanding.

In a witness statement the witness is asked to state whether you have displayed the ability to manage a specific function or core activity successfully and to describe briefly the circumstances under which you did this work. The witness is not generally expected to be familiar with the detailed criteria laid down in professional standards, nor is the witness being asked to make an accurate assessment of your performance (though the relevant parts of the Professional Standard or Framework could be used as a guide).

You should supply the witness with details of the particular items in the Professional Standard/Framework for which the statement is being sought. The witness should describe factually what he/she knows of your work and the circumstances in which it was carried out. The testimony should be written by the witness in a personal capacity based on their personal knowledge of you. It should be typed and on headed paper.

A testimony statement should contain:

- the name of the candidate stated formally as the person being referred to

- the dates when the witness worked with the candidate

- the post or posts held by the candidate and the relationship to the witness at the time

- a list of the competences (functions and core activities) for which the witness is giving evidence

- and a statement of verification, if the witness agrees, and a summary description of the circumstances in which the candidate demonstrated the competences.

Task: Different types of evidence

Identify some sources of direct, indirect and independent evidence that you could include in your portfolio.

Organising evidence

How you will organise your evidence will depend on the type of portfolio you are preparing. Most professional portfolios today are designed to enable a claimant to demonstrate how they meet a set of professional competences, benchmarks, standards or frameworks. Such competences provide an organising structure for a portfolio.

If you do not have professional competences or benchmarks, you may be able to identify key criteria or themes around which you can structure your portfolio. It is important to have clearly defined benchmark statements or themes which your evidence relates to.

Evidence can be integrated as part of an overall portfolio submission or as a set of appendices that follow a reflective commentary. In either case, a summary of evidence, linked to key competences or themes, should be provided at the beginning of the portfolio as a guide for the reader. An example of a Guide to Evidence is provided in Figure 6.3. You will see from the Figure that the Guide to Evidence will provide the reader with a means to navigate their way through the portfolio, seeing where specific competences are met, how this relates to the reflective commentary and the sources of evidence that illustrate this. Note also that the evidence provides a range of direct and indirect sources.

Ethical guidelines for using evidence

In gathering and selecting evidence it is easy to overlook some of the ethical issues associated with using evidence. In this section we discuss some of these issues and explore a number of strategies to ensure that the evidence you include in your portfolio adheres to ethical guidelines and in itself is indicative of your professionalism.

The main issues associated with using evidence in portfolios relate primarily to:

- consent

- collecting evidence

- anonymity.

Consent

Any evidence that involves an individual or group must have received prior consent for inclusion. It is not sufficient to assume that the individuals or groups concerned

Figure 6.3 Example Guide to Evidence

Excellent Teacher Standard

Competence	Case Study Example	Page	Evidence	Page
E7 a) Take a lead in planning collaboratively with colleagues in order to promote effective practice; b) Identify and explore links within and between subjects/curricular areas in their planning. *Professional Standard for Teachers in England (Excellent Teacher) p. 15*	Leader of inter-departmental working party on developing cross curricular themes.	Reflective Commentary, p. 10	Operational Plan (Item 1, Appendix A) Lesson plans devised by group (Item 2, Appendix A) Project Evaluation (Item 3, Appendix A)	p. 36

Advanced Skills Teacher Standard

Competence	Case Study Example	Page	Evidence	Page
A2 Be part of or work closely with leadership teams, taking a leadership role in developing, implementing and evaluating policies and practice in their own and other work places that contribute to school improvement *Professional Standard for Teachers in England (Advanced Skills Teacher) p. 21*	Co-opted to school leadership team to take forward Assessment for Learning in junior school and assist colleagues in implementing DfES guidelines.	p. 34 – p. 38	Minutes of SLT meetings showing participation (Item A, Appendix B) Report to SLT on series of meetings with staff and proposed development plan (Item B, Appendix B) Samples of materials/resources on Assessment for Learning presented to staff during INSET (Item C, Appendix B).	

Standard for Chartered Teacher

Competence	Case Study Example	Page	Evidence	Page
Collaboration with, and influence on, colleagues. *Standard for Chartered Teacher (Scotland) p. 6*	Overview of role as supporter. Mentor for beginning teacher 2007–8	pp. 6–8	Record of meetings with beginning teacher (Item 14, Appendix D) Copy of interim and final report (Item 15, Appendix E) Copy of evaluation completed by beginning teacher on completion of induction year (Item 16, Appendix E) Extracts from learning journal maintained as part of PG course on Mentoring (Item 17, Appendix F).	pp. 20–26

Standard for Headship

Competence	Case Study Example	Page	Evidence	Page
Leading Learning Learning and Teaching	Whole school improvement project on cooperative learning	pp. 4–5	Project plan Evaluation of teacher development programme Pilot study results Project Evalution Report	pp. 31–34

agree to inclusion or even to receive verbal agreement. If your evidence contains reference to another person you must supply evidence of their written consent. The requirement for consent extends to inclusion of all digital, photographic and video materials. A template for a consent form is provided in Figure 6.4.

Gaining consent from classes or large groups of pupils/individuals may be problematic. You should refer to school or local authority policy with regard to this and adhere to this policy. A statement to this effect could also be included in your portfolio.

If you are including as evidence work that you produced when leading or being part of a team or working party, you should seek the consent of the other members of the team/group for its inclusion and acknowledge your contribution, as outlined above.

 Task: Getting consent

Make a list of people you will need to contact or speak to if you will be making reference to them in your portfolio.

Collecting evidence

Most of the evidence you will include will be materials and resources you have generated and which form part of your day-to-day practice or relate to a specific project. However, it might be necessary and appropriate to include other sources of evidence that can verify the claims you are making. As we explored earlier, this evidence can take a range of forms. Care needs to be taken when asking another individual to provide a testimony or witness statement. Providing a template for these may be helpful but dictating or directing their contents is not advisable. Inclusion of selective evaluations from pupils may be appropriate, where they occur as part of the normal learning cycle. Asking pupils to provide evaluations specifically for the portfolio is not generally appropriate.

When involving others in providing testimonials and witness statements it is important to remember the power relationships that can exist between teachers and pupils, lecturers and students, teachers and parents/carers, and possibly line management relationships between teachers and other professionals, and support such as classroom assistants or technicians. Therefore, those involved should be made fully aware that providing a testimonial is optional, that it will be used only for the portfolio and that their anonymity will be protected.

Anonymity

All evidence should be made anonymous and no individual, school or local education authority should be recognisable from the evidence provided unless consent has been given in relation to a specific resource such as video recording. Another exception is independent verification provided in the form of testimonials/witness statements as outlined.

Figure 6.4   Sample consent form

Name and address of workplace

_____

_____

_____

I have been informed by the candidate that their professional portfolio contains references to me in the context of my role as _____

I am happy to agree to this. I understand that my name and/or resources I have developed collaboratively with the candidate will be used only for the purposes of this portfolio.

Name _____

Date _____

Position _____

Photocopiable

Summary

Ensuring evidence is gathered and presented in an ethical way is a measure of the professionalism that the portfolio is designed to show. Approaching evidence-gathering and selection in an ethical way requires professional judgement, and if in doubt, you should consult with a line manager, mentor or critical friend before proceeding.

In this chapter we examined different kinds of evidence:

- direct evidence

- indirect evidence

- independent evidence

We explored specific criteria that you can use to select evidence:

- relevance

- sufficiency

- authenticity

- currency

- competence

We also explored the ethical issues in gathering and presenting evidence:

- consent

- collecting evidence

- anonymity.

7

Describing and Reflecting on Practice

Writing both to describe and then to reflect critically on your practice and learning will be key elements of your professional portfolio. In this chapter we explore some of the different types of writing you might include in a portfolio. To do so we look at a framework that maps out three levels of writing and illustrate each type of writing with some examples.

Key ideas

- **Describing practice**
- **Analysing and evaluating experience**
- **Critical reflective writing**
- **A framework for critical reflective writing**

Writing in a professional portfolio

In a professional portfolio you will be expected to describe and then analyse your practice and learning and so you will have to include different types of writing. A useful way of viewing the different genres of writing you might find in a professional portfolio is to consider three levels of writing:

- *descriptive writing:* providing a clear account of practice

- *evaluative writing:* judging the quality and impact of practice

- *critical reflective writing:* reflecting critically on practice and development and relating these experiences to wider socio-political contexts and the underpinning purposes of education.

We will now consider each type of writing further and explore a number of examples.

Descriptive writing

In descriptive writing the writer focuses on the account of events, the context, the feelings and views of the participants in a situation. For example, the writer might describe a successful direct teaching lesson or a group discussion that was not particularly successful. Clear and detailed descriptive writing is important when you are asked to demonstrate that you have met a particular aspect of a standard or competence framework – what is sometimes referred to as a 'claim for competence'.

Evaluative writing

In evaluative writing the writer focuses on reviewing events and considers any questions, issues and problems that need to be addressed. Here the task is to examine why, for example, the lesson was successful or the group discussion was not successful. The writing is evaluative because judgements are made about the effectiveness of your practice or the decisions you took. Ways of improving practice or possible alternatives are also explored. In this type of writing the elements of the successful lesson to be developed in future lessons would be identified or strategies to improve the use of group discussion would be considered. The focus of evaluative writing remains very much on the specific situation or incident in which you make judgements about the quality of practice and exploring ways of improving this.

Critical reflective writing

In critical reflective writing the writer focuses on placing incidents, situations, practices and experiences in wider contexts. We discussed the importance of wider contexts in the shaping of practice in Chapter 3, where we looked at the professional autobiography. Placing your professional practice in these wider contexts is a key feature of critical reflective writing. Again taking the examples above – direct teaching or group work – these pedagogic approaches would be placed in a wider debate about the nature of effective teaching and learning, for example, discussions about the changing role and place of the learner; a transmission model versus a participative model of learning; the issue of democratic processes in education and the fostering of citizenship.

Examples of writing genres

The short extracts presented here illustrate the three levels of reflective writing: descriptive, evaluative and critical reflective. The question of a group task that was not particularly successful is examined in each extract.

 Task: Examples of reflective writing

As you read through the example extracts, identify and jot down the differences between each piece.

Example: Descriptive writing

I was working with a Year 3 class and the topic was newspaper headlines. Each group was to review the newspapers they had been given and agree upon a set of the most effective headlines. These headlines were then to be displayed and a presentation

(Continued)

(Continued)

prepared to indicate why these headlines had been selected. The class seemed to enjoy the lesson – for the most part they were engaged in reading through the news-papers and collecting headlines. However, they did not work together and were not able to complete the display.

Example: Evaluative writing

The group work on newspaper headlines with Year 3 was not particularly successful. Though initially the pupils seemed to enjoy the task they tended to work individually rather than in their groups. The issue for me now is how to create a genuine group task. There was little relevant discussion though quite a lot of laughter when someone came across a suggestive headline. No group had agreed on five headlines to display. From this group activity there are three key issues I need to consider if I am to develop this approach in my teaching: (1) the design of the task to ensure the pupils have to work together; (2) setting clear expectations for each stage of the task; (3) the pupils' skill in group work.

Example: Critical reflective writing

My predominant mode of teaching with Year 3 has been didactic largely because of control issues. However, such an approach is not helping to develop their ability to read the media critically, an important issue in a media-saturated world. The first group activity was only partially successful – it is clear greater scaffolding is vital but the experi-ence has raised other issues for me about the role of learners. At times I have taken pas-sivity as a sign of attention and now, even though this activity was not fully successful, I have seen, as Johnstone and Johnstone (1994) argue, the potential of pupils learning collaboratively. Though there are some techniques I need to strengthen, this experi-ence has raised for me the question of my values as an educator and my understand-ing of the changing role of the learner. However, this is an issue that we as a department need to consider also because if we are to develop engaged citizens of the future we have to develop trust and provide opportunities consistently so that the pupils can learn productively with their peers.

 Task: Developing reflective writing

Select an issue or episode from your own practice. This could be something that was either: successful or not particularly successful; positive or negative; took place in a short period of time or was an ongoing issue. Use the framework to produce the three types of writing: (1) descriptive, (2) evaluative and (3) critical reflective.

Describing practice: developing an account

One of the purposes of a portfolio is to provide a clear account of specific areas of your practice, whether this is in:

- supporting learning

- teaching

- leading and managing.

There is a need to ensure that you provide sufficient relevant detail so that the account is clear and accurate. However, it is important that you avoid the temptation to 'pad out' this account with activities and tasks that are not relevant to the area of practice you are putting forward. A useful way of starting to gather ideas is to map out the steps and activities in sequence. In the 'Group Work' example you will see the sequence of steps a lecturer took as she worked on a short curriculum development project on group work.

Example: Group work

The question of student participation in seminars was raised as an issue in a recent review:

- discussion in teaching team about developing group work
- gathering material related to group work
- team plans a series of activities to use with students
- information session for students – gathering initial views on programme
- trialling Unit 1
- student review of Unit 1
- review of Unit 1 by teaching team
- trial Unit 2
- student evaluation by questionnaire
- review of evaluation, assessment outcomes and curriculum materials by teaching team

---

The next step is then to select activities relevant to the particular area of practice in which you wish to demonstrate your skill. The lecturer wanted to make a claim for her practice in relation to 'learner's voice' and so needed to select elements from the sequence of steps in the 'Group Work' example and write a descriptive account for the portfolio. This can be found in the 'Developing Learner Voice' example. As you will see, not all the areas or activities listed above are included in this account. It is important that you include what is relevant to the particular area or issue.

Example: Developing learner voice

A key focus for the case study on group discussion was on developing the 'learner voice'. At each stage the views of learners were gathered and used to develop further the material. The first step was to provide an overview of the programme aims and activities and respond to any student concerns. The response from the students was very positive. Briefing materials were discussed and a short review activity was built into each session as well as the more formal gathering of learners' views using an evaluation questionnaire. This material was collated and reported back to the learners. At the end of the term each group representative attended a review meeting to work with the teaching team in reviewing the materials and collated data from the questionnaires. This material was then used by the teaching team to write further Units for next term.

Listing all the steps taken in a project or case study enables you to see the full range of tasks you have undertaken. It can also be used to identify relevant evidence to support a claim. Thus in the next example an aspiring headteacher has selected the relevant steps from his work in building partnerships with parents and then written these up as a claim for competence in 'Building Community'. As part of the claim references are made to specific items of evidence also included in the portfolio.

Example: A claim for competence

- Establish a cross-school short life working group on the homework policy
- Survey of parents
- Consultation with the Parents' Association
- Feedback of outcomes of the surveys
- Letters to parents, newsletter item
- Display for parents' evening
- Proposal to parents for further comments
- Newsletter item
- Parental workshop
- Items on pupil induction programme
- Homework diaries
- Newsletter item 2 – update on project

Claim for competence

I claim competence in building community and will illustrate this through the project on the development of homework. Enhancing parental partnerships was an important outcome of this project. There was an initial presentation to the PA meeting (item 1: presentation notes) about the aims of the project and they agreed to work with the development group to circulate and collect the questionnaires (item 2: meeting notes). They also commented on a draft of the questionnaire. The questionnaire was sent to all parents (item 3: draft and final questionnaire) …

Writing out the steps of a development project, action research project or case study enables you:

- to set out the activities and tasks in sequence

- to match particular aspects to the standard or competence framework or a topic you wish to highlight

- to select relevant evidence to support the case.

Analysing and evaluating practice

Providing a clear account of your practice is important but as you develop this account inevitably you will have to consider what impact your practice has had. Writing an account will also help you to recall issues or queries and to consider some of the strengths and areas for development that have emerged in the course of your work. This then gives you a starting point to evaluate your practice. From this starting point you then need to subject your practice to systematic review against clear criteria. These criteria might be:

- success criteria you identified in a project plan

- outcomes from the relevant standard or competence framework

- performance indicators from a quality assurance framework

- assessment criteria from a programme of study.

Using criteria will enable you to review your practice systematically and rigorously. Again a starting point is to take each criterion and to consider the following:

- Was it achieved?

- How well was it achieved?

- Are there any illustrative examples?

- Are there any gaps or areas for development?

In the example below a lecturer has written some notes to begin evaluating her work on group discussion. She is using the success criteria generated by the working group in planning the development project.

Example: Notes For evaluation	
Criteria	**Notes**
Provide a structured preparatory task to support students' contributions to discussion	Tasks structured & most students prepared; +impact – level of discussion; confidence also in some students – reported felt they had something to say; some tasks better than others at this; just asking students to read an article not as effective as giving guide questions to respond to; noticed many referred to their notes on these questions; need a balance between structured and open-ended; students didn't seem to get as much out of multiple choice tasks, too long & not clearly linked to seminar topic; also comments – questionnaire points to this.

In her notes the lecturer has drawn on her own observations and judgements as well as the data collected throughout the project to consider whether the success criterion has been achieved. This material is then used as part of an evaluation report. An extract from this report is in the next example.

Example: Evaluative writing

Criterion 1
An important strategy in this project was the use of structured tasks to support the students' preparation for each seminar. These tasks varied and included articles, guided questions for reading, short investigations, and multiple-choice questionnaires. Providing a short reading with specific questions to be reflected on was the most successful preparatory task in fostering greater participation during the seminar and this should be continued in the next Unit. The questions were particularly powerful in helping the students to identify and form some views on the key issues to be discussed in the seminar. In other reading tasks where there were no guide questions the students struggled to focus on the key issues in the seminar. Other tasks were far less successful, particularly the multiple choice tasks which had been designed to pose possible alternative views for the students to consider. These tasks were too lengthy and some of the responses not clear. Though some items did provoke some debate, overall the questionnaires could be much briefer ...

In evaluative writing you look closely at and assess the quality of the professional practice. However, this evaluation is very much focused on the specific area of practice in order to consider what might be maintained and what might be modified in future practice. The evaluation of the quality of your practice is an important element in your professional portfolio. However, there are other more fundamental questions that can be asked of your practice and learning as a professional and so we need to consider critical reflective writing.

Critical reflective writing

Critical reflection is a means of probing experiences by considering our actions and behaviours, our motivations, intentions and emotions as an educational practitioner during the experience being examined. This emphasis on the 'full' experience has led to a wide variety of genres being used to reflect, including fiction, poetry, as well as descriptive and critical analytical styles of writing. Bolton (2001: 32) suggests that reflective practice is fostered through 'the looking glass model' of education and critical reflective writing helps us deal with the paradoxes of professional practice, what she calls the:

• certain uncertainty

• serious playfulness

• unquestioning questioning.

In some programmes the use of literary genres is encouraged while in other programmes there is a focus on analytical prose through which you can critically reflect on your practice as an educator. This latter focus is our concern here.

The conception of critical reflection draws from Dewey's (1933) ideas about reflective thinking and Schon's (1983) construction of 'reflection-in-action'. For Dewey reflection is an active process that is both extended and systematic. His term 'severe thought' perhaps gives an indication of some of the challenges reflective thinking can pose for the professional practitioner. Reflective thinking is not only a process that enables us to deal with problems in our practice but it is also a process that helps us define and redefine our value systems. As we reflect critically on an issue or a problem, we have to go back to or make explicit our values that underpin our role as an educational practitioner. Through critical reflection we may also review and refine, and in some instances, revise our values. Critical reflection can also help groups of colleagues who work together to develop a common set of values or at least acknowledge where differences might lie. In this way we, as reflective practitioners, build not just our own knowledge and professional values, but we can also contribute to the values of the professional community.

The term 'critical' refers to the need to look objectively at our practice by measuring it against our values, current understandings about good practice and the wider purposes of education. The term 'critical' suggests the idea of 'critique' in which a critic analyses and evaluates a particular work of art or literature and considers its significance. This idea of critique is a vital part of reflection and professional learning.

Reflecting critically helps us to make sound judgements about our practice in order to gain new insights, to expose and interrogate our underpinning values and also to improve our skill as an educational practitioner. It is important to analyse these experiences against wider educational, social and theoretical concerns. It is this process that helps us to take that imaginative leap into thinking about different possibilities.

In this section you will find a longer example of critical reflective writing, on the subject of pupil behaviour and discipline.

 ## Task: The features of critical reflective writing

As you read the example, identify and note down what you see as the key features of critical reflective writing.

Example: Critical reflective writing

Pupil behaviour and discipline

A pupil who previously had a record of good behaviour was involved in a serious violent incident with another pupil and the follow up interview with the parents raised considerable questions for me as a teacher working in an inner city area, particularly about the role of the school in a specific community and the relationship between the personal and professional values of the practitioners and the communities they work in. Who has the right and responsibility to assert and demand the pursuance of specific values and behaviours?

It was the response of the parents that, on a personal level, stunned me and, on a professional level, made me consider some of my beliefs about the enterprise I am involved in in a public education system. The pupil's parents were of the view that the pupil should not be punished, not because of his previous good behaviour but because he had learned to fight back, something they had been urging him to do. My immediate response was that this was unacceptable, that there were some basic principles that must be abided by in a social context and especially in one such as a school that has a role in the social and personal development of pupils. Further, I also viewed this encouragement as gender-stereotypical thinking in which this pupil was being encouraged to adopt the behaviours that are expected of boys (Jackson, 2002). I was quite clear about my beliefs at this point. However, when the parents indicated their reasons for encouraging their child to fight back – to survive in the neighbourhood which we as teachers 'drove away from at 4 o'clock each afternoon' – I had to question my beliefs. It became a matter of whose values were 'right'. Both the parents and the teachers had the best interests of the pupil at heart. However, in this case the pupil was receiving mixed messages and no matter what course of action he took he would be punished either by his parents' disapproval or by the school's sanctions.

I had interpreted this as a gender issue in which the pupil was being encouraged to behave in a stereotypical way. Partly it was. Certain expectations in the setting the pupil lived in demanded the display of aggression as part of being male. But to characterise this situation as a personal clash of values about gender was too simplistic. There was an issue of the relationship between community and school values and this raised questions about what I saw as the purposes of education. We need to look more closely at a public education system that is not just located in a specific community but

(Continued)

(Continued)

also acts as the means of empowering the pupils and the wider community to act. As Apple and Beane (1995: 11) argue in their discussion about democratic schools:

> their vision [in democratic schools] extends beyond purposes such as improving the school climate or enhancing students' self-esteem. Democratic educators seek not simply to lessen the harshness of social inequities in school, but to change the conditions that create them.

In this piece of writing the scope of the discussion is wider that in the other extracts we have looked at in this chapter. There is a limited description of the circumstances and then the key issue of the clash of values is explored. The focus is not simply on modifying a specific policy or practice in school but on raising questions about attitudes and expectations in education. Different sources, particularly theoretical materials, are drawn upon to highlight specific issues and questions. The tone is more questioning and speculative, leading to a statement of the values position that the educational practitioner believes his practice should be based upon and judged by.

Planning a critical commentary

In a critical commentary you reflect critically on what shaped you as a professional by identifying and exploring a memorable event or issue in your professional career. This might be in relation to a particular project or initiatives or your day-to-day work, whether in teaching or leadership. Here you can look back to Chapter 3, where we developed a framework for exploring your experiences in wider contexts and issues. Part of this discussion in a critical commentary is to locate your experiences within a specific sociopolitical context and to make explicit your underpinning values. In planning a commentary you, firstly, provide a clear description for the reader to understand the setting, episode, issue or event, secondly, you evaluate your practice and, thirdly, you consider wider issues to explore the significance of this situation for your development and future practice.

 Task: Planning a critical commentary

Use Steps 1–3 to develop a critical reflective piece of writing.

- *Step 1*: Think of one memorable event, incident, issue or situation from your recent practice (relating to colleagues or to pupils or students). Write a full description of the event.

- *Step 2*: Review this situation and evaluate the effectiveness of your work: are there aspects of your practice that were successful or not successful, are there aspects you want to enhance or improve, what do you feel you have learned from this situation? What reading material such as theoretical and research material as well as policies and guidelines are available for you to explore good practice?

- *Step 3:*   Think about the following aspects of your own narrative:

What story have you constructed?
How has this shaped you as a professional?
What were the driving forces behind this situation?
What other interpretation of the events could there be?
What reading material and ideas can you draw upon to help you think critically about this situation?
What beliefs and values about education underpin the story?

 Summary

In this chapter we considered a framework that set out three levels of writing:

- descriptive writing

- evaluative writing

- critical reflective writing.

Descriptive writing is appropriate when you are asked to provide a clear and detailed account of your practice as an educational professional. This type of writing is often found in the section of a professional portfolio where you are asked to make claims for competence in relation to aspects or areas specified in a professional standard or competence framework. To help develop your ideas in this type of writing you can draw on material such as policies and guidelines and professional literature that examines practice.

Evaluative writing is important in the portfolio where you are asked to review and judge the effectiveness of your practice and the outcomes you have achieved. In this type of writing it is useful to use criteria to evaluate your practice and to provide sufficient illustration to justify these judgements. These criteria can be generated from theoretical and research literature as well as from policies and guidelines.

Critical reflective writing may be included in a professional portfolio where you are asked to reflect on and critically appraise your development and practice as an educational practitioner. In this type of writing you reflect in depth on specific issues that are central to shaping your development and practice, such as policy, social and political trends, research and questions of the purposes and values underpinning education. Here reading, particularly theoretical and research-based materials, adds a dimension that enables you to explore your practice at this deeper, more critical level.

Designing an Electronic Portfolio

This chapter explores electronic portfolios (e-portfolios) and looks at some of the advantages and opportunities in using an e-format to develop a professional portfolio drawing on the approaches discussed in previous chapters.

Key issues

- **What is an e-portfolio?**
- **Constructing an e-portfolio**
- **The features of an e-portfolio**
- **Using evidence in an e-portfolio**
- **Is an e-portfolio for me?**

Using ICT in developing a portfolio

For most education practitioners, information and communication technology (ICT) is an integral part of their professional practice, both as a resource for learning, teaching and research and as a communicative tool. Enhanced Internet access in both the professional and personal domain means that many practitioners use ICT daily and developing an electronic portfolio is an attractive option for practitioners who operate in electronic contexts as part of their professional work. Developing an e-portfolio requires the same skills of reflective practice that we explored in previous chapters. In addition, it requires a high level of competence in ICT, presenting an opportunity for the practitioner to demonstrate not only the extent of their professional learning but the range of their ICT capability. At this stage you may feel that you have strengths in some areas of ICT but because you are not fully confident in others, an e-portfolio might seem over-ambitious. However, constructing an e-portfolio is a professional development opportunity through which you can acquire, in a purposeful way, further skill in this area, which will add to your own understanding of the potential of ICT in learning and teaching. Constructing an e-portfolio will also give you an opportunity to experiment with different media and to try out different strategies.

E-portfolios are being used much more frequently as teachers progress through their careers. As more professions move towards formal recording and accreditation of professional learning, e-portfolios provide a means for demonstrating this in an accessible and portable way. E-portfolios, in whatever form, provide a great platform for innovation through the use of media such as sound and video in support of your claim. These can, for example, be used as powerful tools to demonstrate a particular approach to your teaching or the dynamic interactions that may take place between educator and learner.

In this chapter we explore:

- what is an electronic portfolio and how it differs from a paper-based portfolio

- how to construct an electronic portfolio

- guidelines for electronic evidence and artefacts

- the advantages and disadvantages of an electronic portfolio.

What is an electronic portfolio?

An electronic or digital portfolio serves the same purpose as a paper-based portfolio except that it is designed, constructed and presented in an electronic format, usually web-based. E-portfolios are becoming increasingly popular and more widely used as portfolios become a central element in recording professional learning, development and practice.

E-portfolios differ primarily from paper-based portfolios in the medium in which they are presented. The electronic medium offers greater opportunity for including a wider variety of audio, digital and graphic resources as well as text. These can also be included in a paper-based portfolio, as CD or DVD discs or CD Roms, whereas in an e-portfolio they can be uploaded or hyperlinked to provide immediate access.

Both types of format are appropriate for the range of purposes of professional portfolios outlined in Chapter 1 (course portfolio, CPD portfolio, competence-based portfolio, accreditation portfolio, project portfolio). While changes and additions can be made to both paper-based portfolios and e-portfolios, the latter provides the opportunity to do so without the need to reformat and reprint the portfolio.

How to construct an electronic portfolio

The same principles and stages of portfolio design and construction that we have explored in previous chapters apply in the design and construction of an e-portfolio. These include:

- understanding professional learning and recording it

- using frameworks for professional learning to reflect critically on practice

- developing a professional biography and career timeline

- critical reflection and writing.

Figure 8.1 Portfolio design and construction

> ➤ *Planning*   How is learning planned and how are the important dimensions of professional learning in the work context to be identified?
> ➤ *Practice*   What frameworks can be used to chart practice and development?
> ➤ *Gathering evidence*   What counts as evidence?
> ➤ *Selecting evidence*   How is relevant and appropriate evidence selected?
> ➤ *Reflecting*   What are some of the ways to reflect critically on practice and development?

The questions you have to ask at each stage of the design and construction process are summarised in Figure 8.1.

However, there are several additional questions to consider when you are intending to construct an e-portfolio. These include:

• What will be the electronic medium for the portfolio?

• Are you confident and competent to design and construct an e-portfolio?

• How is the electronic material to be organised?

• Who will need to access the portfolio and when?

We consider each of these questions below.

What will be the electronic medium for the portfolio?

There are several options available for constructing an e-portfolio and generally these are web-based. One option may be to design a personal website that will serve as your professional portfolio. Another option is to use a web-based platform such as Blackboard, WebCT, PeddlePad or Moodle (web addresses are provided at the end of this chapter). The portfolio could also be presented on CD Rom combining text and digital images. There is also a range of commercial packages available on-line. At the end of this chapter we provide links for two examples of professional portfolios designed to meet the competences for a Certificate in Academic Practice.

You will need to ensure that you have server facilities to host your e-portfolio. You do not need to know much about complex programming languages such as HTML (Hypertext Markup Language) to develop an e-portfolio as there are large numbers of user-friendly packages such as Adobe Dreamweaver™ that have been developed to support non-expert website design.

If you opt to develop a personal website for your portfolio, the usability of your website can be affected by a limited understanding of good practice in web design, particularly in relation to the navigation between individual web pages and documents. It is worth investing time in developing your website architecture at the start of the development process in order to outline the document structure for your website. It is also worth carrying out some rudimentary testing to ensure that the user-interface is intuitive for non-specialist users. Further information on good practice in web design can be found at www.useit.com/.

You may already have access to existing electronic platforms or they may be used within your organisation. It is a good idea to speak to colleagues who may have already developed an e-portfolio and to seek advice from an ICT adviser or specialist. You may also find it helpful to spend some time researching the options available to you and to look at examples of e-portfolios. There is a range of e-portfolios that can be accessed via the Internet and while some may not be relevant to your specific requirements, they do nevertheless exemplify the possibilities in e-portfolio development. The following website provides open access to e-portfolios: http://electronicportfolios.com/ALI/samples.html.

Are you confident and competent to design and construct an e-portfolio?

An e-portfolio is an attractive option for those who feel confident about and are competent in using ICT. It is important that you have the necessary skills for designing and constructing an e-portfolio or will have the opportunity to acquire and develop these skills as you embark on your portfolio. It is also important to have access to the technology and software you will require for developing the portfolio and if possible the support of an ICT adviser should you require assistance. Opting to present a professional portfolio in an electronic or digital format requires careful consideration and judgement as to whether your ICT competence is at an appropriate level or for the present time is better suited to preparing a paper-based portfolio. Nevertheless, designing and compiling an e-portfolio presents an opportunity to acquire and enhance existing skills and to acquire new approaches that will not only add to your portfolio but your practice as an educator so that designing and compiling an e-portfolio becomes a professional development opportunity.

How is the electronic material to be organized?

The materials presented in an electronic portfolio are broadly similar to the materials in a paper-based portfolio and will include text and digital material. The structure will also be broadly similar to the structure for a paper-based portfolio, though for an e-portfolio the organisation does not need to be linear. A list of the generic features of portfolios is found in Figure 8.2.

While e-portfolios do not need to have a linear organisation, they do nevertheless require a logical order and so it is important to design and provide a navigational aid for users. This is also the case for paper-based portfolios, where the planning stage is a central part of putting together the portfolio.

E-portfolios provide the opportunity for linking between several items of text and digital resources. Important questions to consider are how these are to be integrated, for example, as hyperlinks or in PDF format. E-portfolios can range from simply a set of documents, similar to those in a paper portfolio, posted on to a website and organised around a table of contents whose items are linked to relevant sets of relevant information and materials (Kahn in Seldin, 2004: 37), to more a more sophisticated version that optimises multi media (2004: 38). E-portfolios offer the opportunity to include a greater range of evidence/artifacts: 'if it can be digitised then it can go in an e-portfolio' (Gomez, 2004).

Figure 8.2   Generic features of portfolios

> ➤ Introduction
>
> ➤ Claims for competence (cross referenced to evidence)
>
> ➤ Reflective commentary
>
> ➤ Evidence (annotated)
>
> ➤ Conclusion (summary of key themes/next steps)
>
> ➤ Bibliography and references

Who will need to access the portfolio and when?

Depending on the purpose of your professional portfolio you will need to determine who will be able to access your e-portfolio. Many e-portfolios are open access but generally those developed for assessment or accreditation will have restricted access in the first instance. If this is the case, you will need to determine how to provide access for assessors (for example, using a protected password) and for how long. You may decide to provide open access for your portfolio and if this is the case you will need to consider issues of ethical compliance, consent and copyright (these are discussed below).

An e-portfolio is an exciting and dynamic way of developing and recording professional learning. However, opting for this form of a portfolio requires careful consideration relating to issues of access to appropriate hardware and software, ICT competence and access and security. You may find it helpful to complete the next task to inform your decision on the type of portfolio you will opt for.

Figure 8.3   Evidence/artefacts for e-portfolios (adapted from Gomez, 2004)

> ➤ Word or text documents
>
> ➤ PowerPoint presentations
>
> ➤ Web pages with hyperlinks
>
> ➤ Excel spreadsheets and graphs
>
> ➤ Scanned images
>
> ➤ Digital photographs
>
> ➤ Multimedia audio and video files
>
> ➤ Results from interactive computer-assessment programs

 Task: Should I use an e-portfolio format?

Working through the questions (in Figure 8.4) will help you to consider whether an e-format would be a suitable approach to use in the development of your professional portfolio.

Figure 8.4   Planning an e-portfolio

Key questions	Questions to ask yourself
What will be the electronic medium for the portfolio?	➢ Am I familiar with designing webpages? ➢ Can I access WebCT, PebblePad or Moodle? Who can advise me?
Are you confident and competent to design and construct an e-portfolio?	➢ Do I have sufficient ICT skills? ➢ Can I convert documents into PDF formats? ➢ Can I digitise artefacts? ➢ Can I upload digital artefacts? ➢ Do I have access to ICT support?
How is the electronic material to be organised?	➢ Do I have a broad plan for the portfolio? ➢ Are there clear guidelines for me to follow or will I have to design my own plan?
Who will need to access the portfolio and when?	➢ Do I know who will require access to the portfolio, such as my employer, accreditation body, assessors, administrative staff, colleagues? ➢ How will access be managed?

Guidelines for electronic evidence and artefacts

In Chapter 6 we provided detailed guidance on collecting and selecting good evidence. You should refer to Chapter 6 when considering material for inclusion as evidence in an e-portfolio. Here we provide a summary of the key factors to keep in mind when thinking about evidence for your portfolio and explore a number of these factors specifically in relation to e-portfolios.

Helpful criteria in selecting evidence are:

- *Relevance:* directly related to the claims being made in the portfolio, both in terms of content and chronology

- *Sufficiency:* adequate in quality, quantity and range to clearly exemplify the claims being made in the portfolio

- *Authenticity:* reflecting your own work or work that you have contributed to, and capable of independent verification

- *Currency:* reflecting current practice, generally within the past three years, often no more than five years and only exceptionally more than five

- *Competence:* demonstrating effective and ethically sound practice and the achievement of successful outcomes, evidenced in monitoring and evaluation.

Using evidence ethically

Educators increasingly are using ICT as a central part of their practice and there are clearly a number of benefits to designing and constructing an e-portfolio. E-portfolios provide practitioners with the opportunity to present their learning and development in imaginative and creative ways. Existing resources, for example a PowerPoint presentation or a podcast, can be uploaded and hyperlinked with relative ease. A lesson or meeting could be digitally recorded, uploaded and accompanied by a reflective commentary via a podcast or audio file. Resources can be updated or additional commentary provided without reproducing the entire portfolio.

As the opportunities for including artefacts extend, it is important to ensure that materials and resources that are included in an e-portfolio adhere to ethical guidelines. An effective recording and tracking system for ethical approval is needed as e-portfolios offer the opportunity to change content and resources more rapidly and frequently than a paper-based portfolio.

In Chapter 6 we considered the key principles for using evidence in a portfolio. We will summarise the main points below but you may find it helpful to re-read the relevant section in Chapter 6.

When including evidence or artefacts in a professional portfolio the main issues relate to:

- *Consent:* any evidence that involves an individual or group must have received prior consent for inclusion. In an e-portfolio written consent can be included as text or digitised resource. You may be including a testimony from your line manager or a colleague as a podcast or audio file. If so, it is important that they clearly state that they are happy for the resource to be used for the purpose of the portfolio and that they know and understand its purpose and who will have access to it. Similarly if using a digital recording that involves children or adults, consent should be received in advance and should be noted either as part of the recording or as a separate file. This is a critical issue, especially if you intend to allow open access to your portfolio.

- *Collecting evidence*: most of the evidence you will include will be materials and resources you have generated and form part of your area of practice but you should also include other sources of evidence that can verify the claims you are making, for example, a testimony or witness statement. It is important those involved are fully aware that providing a testimonial is optional and will be used only for the portfolio. If you are including materials or artefacts that were generated as part of team effort or collaboration, your specific contribution should be noted and those involved should give their consent for the work to be included and their role to be acknowledged. The sample consent form in Chapter 6 can be easily adapted for this.

- *Anonymity:* all evidence should be made anonymous and no individual, school or local education authority should be recognisable from the evidence provided unless consent has been given in relation to a specific resource such as video recording. Another exception is independent verification provided in the form of testimonials/ witness statements as outlined above and discussed in detail in Chapter 6.

As we noted above it is important to have an effective recording and tracking system for consent and ethical approval for evidence and artefacts included in a portfolio. For each piece of evidence you intend to include you should note who is involved, whether consent is required, when consent was received and a record of where the consent is currently located or will be located in the e-portfolio.

Figure 8.5 shows an example of a record sheet for recording and tracking consent. This could be included as a separate file in the portfolio.

What are the advantages and disadvantages of an electronic portfolio?

There are many advantages in producing an e-portfolio. E-portfolios are easier to change and update and so are more dynamic and live than paper-based portfolios. In this respect e-portfolios, especially those that are maintained and updated regularly, can capture a more dynamic sense of ongoing professional learning and development than paper-based portfolios that provide a record to a certain point.

E-portfolios offer the opportunity for a more personalised approach in which the educational practitioner's perspective can be reflected at the same time as meeting the range of criteria for the portfolio. E-portfolios also offer the potential for a greater degree of interactivity than is possible with paper-based portfolios and potentially with a greater range of users.

Ease of access, from a user's perspective, is clearly one of the advantages of the e-portfolio and the portfolio can be linked to other aspects of professional practice such as an institutional or organisational website or virtual learning environment.

There are, however, some potential disadvantages associated with e-portfolios. Referring to teaching portfolios, Kahn (2004) warns that 'perhaps the greatest challenge for creators of electronic teaching portfolios is the danger of overwhelming readers with excessive, badly organised, or uninterrupted information' (2004: 43). The same is also true for all portfolios and not only teaching portfolios, and equally the danger of 'information overload' is relevant for paper-based as well as e-portfolios. Particular care is needed, however, in the design and organisation of text and evidence to enable the reader/user of an e-portfolio to navigate with ease.

Scanning and digital imaging means that many sources used by education practitioners can be uploaded to a website, though the choice of an e-portfolio may preclude the inclusion of some artefacts. However, alternative ways of representing the artefact can be considered, such as a series of still photographs or a short digital film of its production.

Putting together an e-portfolio is a rewarding but challenging task and so it is important to fully consider the benefits of designing an e-portfolio from a personal perspective. Without the necessary ICT skills and competence there is a danger that the task may become overly time-consuming and so at the outset you should think about the skills you have and what you might need to develop. Also think about what support or development opportunities might be available for you to acquire skills and understanding.

E-portfolios offer the potential to incorporate a range of evidence of professional learning and development in creative and imaginative ways that can be added to and enhanced. Because of the range of opportunities associated with this, careful selection of evidence, adherence to ethical guidelines and procedures and systematic recording of consent and approval for inclusion are important. With this in mind, in the next section we examine two sample e-portfolios.

Figure 8.5a Record Sheet

	Item of evidence/ artefact	Individuals involved	Nature of activity	Type of consent	Date consent received	Location of record of consent
Example 1	Digital recording of small group reading intervention with P3 pupils	10 P3 pupils Classroom assistant Classroom teacher (self)	20 minute group activity based on reading intervention developed and designed by self Classroom assistant assisted with paired and group activities linked to intervention	Parental consent request for 10 pupils Written consent requested from CA Headteacher's consent for inclusion of artefact in portfolio	All parental consent received by 20/09/07 18/09/07 24/09/07	Consent file – hard copy
Example 2	Minutes of Departmental Meeting	7 members of teaching staff; 2 classroom assistants; Learning Support teacher (peripatetic)	Departmental Meeting with focus on developing formative assessment strategies Inclusion of Minutes reflects discussion, distribution of tasks and timeline	Written consent from all participants at meeting	28/08/07	Consent file – hard copy

Photocopiable

Putting Together Professional Portfolios. SAGE © Christine Forde, Margery McMahon & Jenny Reeves, 2009.

Figure 8.5b   Record Sheet Blank Version

	Item of evidence/ artefact	Individuals involved	Nature of activity	Type of consent	Date consent received	Location of record of consent

Photocopiable

Figure 8.6   Example e-portfolio: screen shot 1

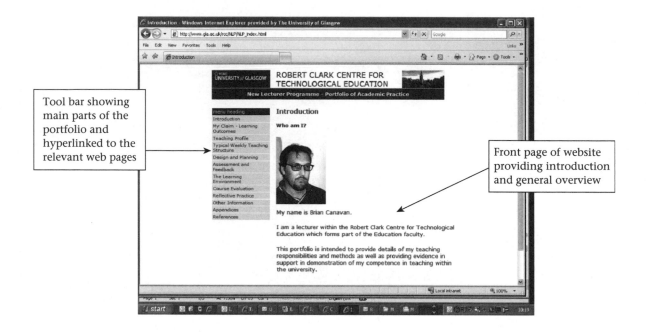

Example e-portfolios

Screen shots

Screen shot 1 is a sample of a web-based portfolio designed to meet the requirements of the New Lecturer Programme at the University of Glasgow. The portfolio is the means by which participants provide evidence of their achievement and basic competence in the learning outcomes of the NLP and provide a critically reflective account of their practice (NLP Guidelines). The portfolio is presented in two parts. The first part provides a reflective account summarising the participant's approach, practice and future plans as an academic practitioner. The second part is an organised collection of evidence presented in order to support the claims the participant is making about his/her practice.

In screen shot 2 the actual claim for competence is made, based on the specific learning outcomes of the programme of study. Screen shot 3 shows the Appendices that are provided to support the claims for competence made in the portfolio.

Screen shot 4 demonstrates an electronic portfolio for the Certificate in Electronic Practice using Moodle as a platform. Moodle is an open source course management system (Cole, 2005). This electronic portfolio is structured around the Learning Outcomes of the programme of study. Each topic heading refers to a specific learning outcome. This is shown in screen shot 5.

Within Moodle, evidence can be uploaded as text, a web link to a document or a hyperlink. Screen shot 6 illustrates how links to evidence are incorporated as part of the commentary on a specific learning outcome or benchmark.

Figure 8.7   Example e-portfolio: screen shot 2

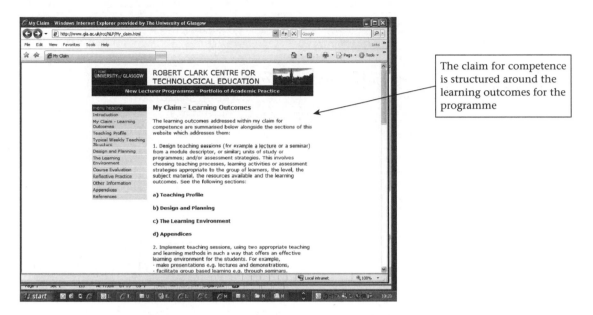

Figure 8.8   Example e-portfolio: screen shot 3

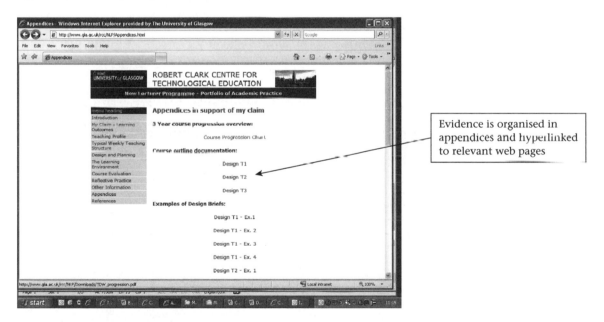

Resources for the development of an electronic portfolio

Sample sites on-line

- http://electronicportfolios.com/ALI/samples.html (accessed 13 June 2008)

- www.gla.ac.uk/rcc/NLP/NLP_index.html (accessed 13 June 2008)

E-portfolios

You may find it helpful to consult the following sites when considering opting for an e-portfolio:

Figure 8.9   Example e-portfolio: screen shot 4

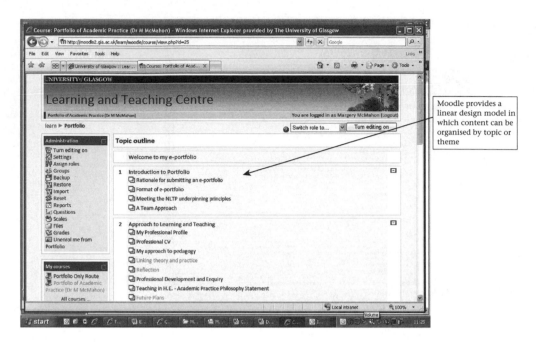

- http://electronicportfolios.com/ALI/samples.html (accessed 13 June 2008)

- www.useit.com/ (accessed 13 June 2008)

- Blackboard and WebCT: www.blackboard.com/us/index.bbb (accessed 13 June 2008)

- PebblePad: www.pebblelearning.co.uk/ (accessed 13 June 2008)

- Moodle: www.moodle.org/ (accessed 13 June 2008)

Figure 8.10   Example e-portfolio: screen shot 5

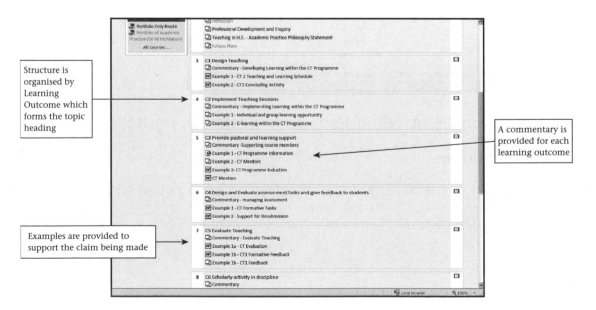

Figure 8.11 Example of e-portfolio: screen shot 6

General commentary

Brief commentary on examples to illustrate practice with a hyperlink to specific evidence object

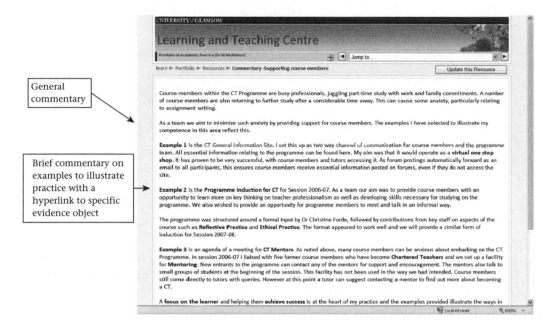

Summary

E-portfolios, in whatever form, provide a great platform for innovation through the use of media such as sound and video in support of your claim. These can, for example, be used as powerful tools to demonstrate your skill in using particular strategies or approaches in your teaching or to depict interactions that may take place between educator and learner in your classroom.

In this chapter we looked at:

- the main principles and stages involved in designing an e-portfolio
- possible formats for an e-portfolio
- and the range of evidence that can be included in an electronic portfolio.

We explored some factors to consider if opting for an e-portfolio such as:

- the electronic medium best suited to your e-portfolio
- competence to undertake an electronic portfolio
- organising material in an electronic format
- managing open or restricted access to the portfolio.

Finally, we looked at how to use evidence effectively in an electronic portfolio and ways to ensure that electronic evidence adheres to ethical guidelines, including issues of consent, evidence collection and anonymity.

9

Designing and Constructing Your Portfolio

In this final chapter we draw together a number of the key ideas explored in the previous chapters and consider ways of designing and constructing your professional portfolio to plan and demonstrate your professional development as an educational practitioner.

Key issues

- the generic features of a portfolio
- planning a portfolio
- guidelines for preparing your portfolio

In this book we have defined a professional portfolio as a means of structuring, demonstrating and reflecting on your development and a tool for providing evidence that you have learned to change and develop your practice in the context of your day-to-day work.

In previous chapters we explored a range of skills and approaches that can assist in preparing a professional portfolio. These are:

- understanding professional learning and recording it

- using frameworks for professional learning to reflect critically on practice

- developing a professional biography and career timeline

- critical reflection and writing.

In this chapter we will review these, drawing together the key ideas to help plan the portfolio.

Generic features of a professional portfolio

As we noted in Chapter 1, portfolios can serve a variety of purposes and this will determine the format of the portfolio. However, generic features for most portfolios include the following features:

- Introduction

- Claims for competence (cross-referenced to evidence)

- Reflective commentary

- Evidence

- Conclusion

- Bibliography and references

If you have completed the accompanying tasks as you read through the previous chapters you should now have a clearer idea of:

- Why you want to develop a portfolio

- The purpose of your portfolio

- The nature of your portfolio.

Selecting your material

The first step is to decide what areas or aspects of your practice you wish to include in your professional portfolio. In your discussion of your professional practice and claim for competence you will draw on examples from practice to exemplify or illustrate your practice. How many examples you should include will depend on the guidelines for submission. For example, for the professional portfolio for Chartered Teacher Accreditation, three case studies or 'critical incidents' are suggested. In programmes for aspiring headteachers, course participants reflect on a whole-school development project they have led. Clearly such case studies should be carefully chosen to best reflect the claim for competence you are making. The elements of professional learning we considered in Chapter 2 provide you with strategies that you can use for reflecting on significant professional learning experiences. Skills for developing reflective thinking, explored in Chapter 4, such as learning journals, elicitation or critical incident analysis, will help you identify the case studies or examples that clearly exemplify your claim for competence.

As we noted above, the case studies, projects or examples from practice you include should be carefully selected as good illustrations of your practice in this area or competence. Their selection and inclusion should be explained clearly. While it is necessary to describe what you did, the focus should be more on explaining your motivation for your approach or actions and reflecting critically on the process and its outcomes. A helpful strategy for reviewing a case study/critical incident is the 'action–review cycle', reflecting on an activity using the following headings:

- Auditing

- Planning

- Implementation

- Monitoring

- Evaluation

So to begin ...

Drawing on your reading from the previous chapters you will now be able to develop the main parts of your portfolio. In this section we offer guidelines for designing and constructing each element of the portfolio.

Introduction

The introduction should provide an overview and be a guide for the reader/assessor to navigate the portfolio. A contents page or brief guide to the layout of the portfolio is always very useful for the reader. As well as providing a summary of the main areas of focus, linked to a professional standard or competence framework (if appropriate), the introduction can also include a short overview of your professional context and career. A shortened form of the professional biography and career timeline discussed in Chapter 4 could be included here.

Claims for competence (cross-referenced to evidence)

This part of the portfolio should include a clear statement of the claims for competence linked to:

- professional standards or competence (if relevant)

- examples, projects or case studies from practice that you have included

- evidence to support the claim.

It should be clear from this section of your portfolio how each of the case studies/examples relates to the professional standards/competences that you are seeking to meet. This can be done either by using the professional standards/competences as headings or by referring to them directly in the course of your discussion or making reference to specific claims for competence.

This section should also have clear links to the evidence you have provided in support of the claim you are making. This should be referenced in the course of the discussion, either by providing the page reference or appendix number in parenthesis or by providing a brief explanation, for example:

> *This is evidenced by Item 4, Appendix B (Minutes of Working Party on Assessment) which shows the agreed plan of implementation for review of assessment.*

Reflective commentary

The reflective commentary forms a key part of the portfolio. Here you will outline and explain in greater depth the claims you are making for professional competence. There is a variety of ways to approach this, and this will depend on the guidelines you have been given for submission of your portfolio. For example, you may use the benchmarks or competences from a professional standard to organise this section.

Central to this section is a discussion of your professional practice, using examples to illustrate your claims for competence or enhanced practice. The discussion should be based on critical self-evaluation and reflection, through which you demonstrate how you have changed and developed as a practitioner, the processes associated with this, how this has shaped your current practice and how it may impact on it in the future.

The skills and strategies we explored in previous chapters will be helpful to you in constructing this section of your portfolio.

- In Chapter 3 the discussion on the professional autobiography and career time-line will help you to demonstrate how you have changed and developed as a practitioner.

- In Chapter 4 the approaches for critical reflection will provide you with strategies to analyse and interpret the processes of change and development you have experienced, as well as helping you to think prospectively.

- In Chapter 5 we explored different ways of reflecting and these can be used to generate material and ideas in order to review and plan your practice.

- In Chapter 6 we considered different types of writing and the tasks you completed in that chapter will have demonstrated to you how to use these. It is likely that you will use all three types of writing (descriptive, evaluative and critically reflective) in this section, though it is the latter that will be most important.

In your critical reflection on a case study, project or activity, you may make appropriate reference to relevant research/literature, to situate your professional practice in the wider context of professional literature in your field and to demonstrate how your practice and experience are understood in relation to key themes and issues. For portfolios that are part of programmes of study, this is often a required element. Guidance on referencing is provided later in this chapter.

Evidence

As you have read through this book you will have understood the importance of supporting claims for competence with appropriate evidence. In Chapter 7 we explored the different types of evidence that might be included in a portfolio and looked at criteria for selecting evidence. These are summarised again for you here:

- Relevance

- Sufficiency

- Authenticity

- Currency

- Competence

You should apply these criteria when selecting evidence for your portfolio, ensuring that you provide *a range of evidence* and are not overly reliant on one or two types of evidence. Remember too that one quality piece of evidence such as a comprehensive project evaluation report can be used to demonstrate that you are meeting several competences/bench marks.

Evidence can be organised in the order in which it is referred to in the reflective commentary, making it easier for readers to navigate their way through the portfolio. Evidence relevant to particular case studies or examples can be organised into appendices. Items of evidence should be labelled (for example Item A or Item 1) and match the reference in the reflective commentary. Evidence should also be briefly annotated, making clear what it is, what it relates to and what it exemplifies (for example, Item C: Extract from Learning Journal; Case Study 2 – CPD course on Additional Support Needs, showing reflection and planning as a result of course).

In Chapter 6 we considered the ethical issues associated with including evidence in a professional portfolio. When constructing your portfolio it is important to adhere to ethical guidelines relating to consent, anonymity and collecting evidence.

Conclusion

Your professional portfolio should include a short conclusion in which you briefly restate your claim for competence, summarising succinctly the basis for this, related to the key themes arising from the reflective commentary and providing some indication of how you will continue to develop your professional practice in these and other areas.

Bibliography and references

In the final part of your portfolio you should provide a list of all sources you have referred to in your portfolio. This should be organised according to an appropriate referencing system. Your guidelines for submission should provide you with information about this. The Harvard system is the most widely used form of referencing. Guidance relating to Harvard referencing is provided in the next section of this chapter.

Guidelines for preparing your professional portfolio

In this section we provide some guidelines on preparing your portfolio for submission. We will look at three main areas: organisation, presentation and submission. We also provide a checklist you can use before you make your final submission. As a starting point we will look at some sample contents listings of different portfolios. The format and presentation for your portfolio may be clearly specified or it might be up to you to determine how you will organise and present the portfolio. Whether your portfolio has a set format or whether you can design this, a useful starting point is to draw up a contents page. This will give you an overall structure around which you can then write or gather specific material.

Example structure 1

Portfolio for School Leadership Development Programme

Personal Learning Plan
Aims and Success Criteria of School Development Project
Project Plan
Project Evaluation Report
Claims for Competence
Reflective Commentary
Evidence

Example structure 2

Portfolio for Classroom Enquiry Course

Contents
Aims and Rationale for Classroom Enquiry
Methodology
Presentation and Analysis of Findings
Critical Reflection on My Learning
Conclusion
Investigative Tools
Summary Data

The nature of your final submission will depend on formal guidelines for submission and on the specific purpose of your portfolio. For portfolios that are to be assessed, there will usually be a set of published assessment criteria and you should ensure that you are familiar with these and refer to them frequently as you prepare your portfolio. If you are uncertain about any of the criteria, seek advice from a tutor or colleague.

Organisation

Putting together a professional portfolio, especially for accreditation, can be very time-consuming and so it is important to have an organised approach, both to the materials you will use and how you will manage your time.

You will have identified the date for submission and you may find it helpful to devise a plan or timeline to help you work towards that date. It may be useful to speak to other colleagues who have successfully completed a portfolio to discuss their approach. If exemplars of the type of portfolio you are expected to produce are available you should spend some time reviewing one or two of these. In your timeline for your project you should factor in time for collecting and collating evidence and for proof reading the entire portfolio prior to submission. It is wise to over-estimate rather than under-estimate the time needed for this, which may help avoid last-minute panic.

You will have accumulated a large amount of resources in the course of preparing your portfolio. How you will organise these will depend on the type of your portfolio but they can be organised thematically or by using professional standards/ benchmarks as headings. Guidelines for submission should give you an indication of the main items that should be included in your portfolio. As your resources accumulate it is helpful to organise them in a file or database. Most portfolios contain a list of contents and a list of evidence and you can compile and update this list as you prepare your portfolio.

Presentation

Portfolios can be presented in a variety of formats and this will be linked to the type of portfolio you are preparing. One option is an e-portfolio, which we considered in Chapter 8. If you opt for a paper-based submission, you will need to decide on how you will present it. Most paper-based portfolios are presented in lever arch files, making it easy to insert or remove materials.

Guidelines for submission should provide you with details relating to word length, font and font size and an appropriate referencing system, as any sources that you refer to should be referenced. One of the most commonly used systems is the Harvard or author–data system. For example, using Harvard referencing you would cite a source you have used as, e.g., (Seldin, 2004) in the course of your text. If you are quoting directly, you must provide the appropriate page reference, as in (Seldin, 2004: 61). You then provide the full citation in a list, as a bibliography or list of references, at the end of your document. The full citation for a source contains the author's name, year of publication, title of the publication, place of publication and the publisher. For example, Seldin, P. (2004) *The Teaching Portfolio*. Bolton: Anker.

Submission

You should ensure that you are familiar with the guidelines for submission of your portfolio. In addition to confirming the time and date of submission you should check if more than one copy of the portfolio is required and whether you will need to provide any accompanying documentation.

Pre-submission checklist

Prior to submission you should allocate time to proof read the portfolio and to make any necessary changes. You may also find it helpful to review the portfolio using the criteria for assessment. You should also do a final check before submission to ensure you have included all necessary elements and addressed all the procedural criteria. The checklist in Figure 9.1 may assist you with this.

Figure 9.1 Pre-submission checklist

		Yes/No
Contents Are the following included	Table of contents	
	List of acknowledgements	
	List of evidence	
	Introduction	
	Claim for competence	
	Reflective commentary	
	Conclusion	
	Bibliography/list of references	
Evidence Is the evidence	Numbered/labelled	
	Annotated	
	Matched to reference in text	
	Anonymous	
Procedural criteria	Within word length	
	Appropriate font and size	
	Checked for grammar, spelling and punctuation	

Photocopiable

A final word

Designing and constructing a professional portfolio can at times be a frustrating and messy task. However, it is worth remembering that this process is developmental, that as you review and reflect on your experiences you are gaining new insights into your professional practice and new confidence in your role as an educational practitioner. At the heart of the process is not simply the creation of a neatly presented portfolio (though that is important – especially for your readers) but instead this is portfolio-based learning which is a sense-making process. You can look at the construction of a portfolio as a process of making meaning. As you plan, review and reflect on your progress and learning as an educational practitioner you gain an understanding of your own professional growth which will help you think more deeply about the process of learning in whatever educational context your work.

A final word: from our experience of working with many different groups of educational practitioners, we know that the task of constructing a professional portfolio, though challenging, is rewarding!

References

Ball, S. (2003) 'The teacher's soul and the terrors of performativity', *Journal of Education Policy*, 18 (2): 215–228.

Bolton, G. (2001) *Reflective Writing for Professional Development*. London: Sage.

Cole, J. (2005) *Using Moodle: Teaching with Popular Open Source Course Management System*. Sebastopol, CA: O'Reilly Media.

Day, C., Sammons, P., Stobart, G., Kigton, A. and Gu, Q. (2007) *Teachers Matter: Connecting Lives, Work and Effectiveness*. Maidenhead: Open University Press.

Department for Children, Schools and Families (2007) *Professional Standards for Teachers in England*, from www.teachernet.gov.uk/ (accessed 10 October 2007).

Dewey, J. (1933) *How We Think: A Re-statement of the Relationship of Reflective Thinking to Learning*. New York: Heath.

Dreyfus, H. L. and Dreyfus, S. E. (1986) *Mind Over Machine: The Power of Human Intuition and Expertise in the Era of the Computer*. Oxford: Blackwell.

Eraut, M. (1994) *Developing Professional Knowledge and Competence*. London: The Falmer Press.

Forde, C., McMahon, M., McPhee, A. and Patrick, F. (2006) *Professional Development, Reflection and Enquiry*. London: Paul Chapman.

General Teaching Council Scotland (2006) *The Standard for Full Registration*. Edinburgh: The General Teaching Council of Scotland.

Gomez, S. (2004) 'Electronic portfolios in Higher Education', Higher Education Academy, from www.heacademy.ac.uk/resources/detail/id446_electronic_portfolios (accessed 29 September 2007).

Hopkins, D. (2002) *Improving the Quality of Education for All: A Handbook of Staff Development Activities*. London: David Fulton.

Hopkins, D., West, M. and Ainscow, M. (1996) *Improving the Quality of Education for All*. London: David Fulton.

Joyce, B. and Showers, B. (1988) *Student Achievement through Staff Development*. London: Longman.

Lewin, K. (1952) 'Group decision and social change', in G. E. Swanson, T. N. Newcomb and E. L. Hardley (eds), *Readings in Social Psychology*. New York: Holt.

Lorenzo, G. and Ittelson, J. (2005) 'An overview of e-portfolios', from www.educause.edu/ir/library/pdf/ELI3001.pdf (accessed 10 December 2007).

Rippon, J. (2005) 'Re-defining careers in education', *Career Development International*, 10 (4): 275–292.

Ross, J. (2006) *E-portfolios for Scotland's Teachers – Background Paper*, from http://erdee.org.uk/natsem/eport_seminar_background.pdf (accessed 10 December 2007).

Sachs, J. (2003) *The Activist Teaching Profession*. Buckingham: Open University Press.

Schon, D. (1983) *The Reflective Practitioner*. Aldershot: Ashgate Arena.

Scottish Executive (2002) *The Standard for Chartered Teacher*. Edinburgh: The Stationery Office.

Scottish Executive (2004) *Ambitious, Excellent Schools: Our Agenda for Action*. Edinburgh: Scottish Executive.

Seldin, P. (2004) *The Teaching Portfolio*. Bolton: Anker.

Stefani, L., Mason, R. and Pegler, C. (2007) *The Educational Potential of E-portfolios*. Abington: Routledge.

Training and Development Agency for Schools (2007) *Professional Standards for Teachers (post-qualification level) Core*. London: Training and Development Agency for Schools.

Tripp, D. (1993) *Critical Incidents in Teaching: Developing Professional Judgement*. London: Routledge.

Western SQH Consortium (2006) *360 Feedback Questionnaire*. Glasgow: Western Scottish Qualification for Headship Consortium.

Index

Added to a page number 'f' denotes a figure.